Chelsea & Matt:
You are now
greatest mi
Creation, hi
son. May you all be blessed for
years & years to come!
Wendy

Create Your Miraculous Life

It's Never Too Late

Wendy L. Darling

Crescendo
PUBLISHING

Create Your Miraculous Life: It's Never Too Late
By Wendy Darling

Crescendo Publishing, LLC
2-558 Upper Gage Ave., Ste. 246
Hamilton, ON L8V 4J6
Canada

GetPublished@CrescendoPublishing.com
1-877-575-8814

ISBN: 978-1-948719-31-5 (P)
ISBN: 978-1-948719-32-2 (E)

Printed in the United States of America

Cover Design by Graphic3ddesign

10 9 8 7 6 5 4 3 2 1

Dedication

To my father, Nelson Lackritz. Your Hebrew name of "Nissan," which translates to "miracle," guided me to create a foundation of believing in the miracles of life, especially at a time when my life was feeling extremely un-miraculous. I will be forever grateful that I was blessed you were my dad.

To my mom, Gladys "Jeff" Lazarow. More than any other person on this planet, you were most instrumental to me growing into the woman I have become. The lessons were not always easy. And your example of growth also showed me how it's truly "never too late" to experience anything you want in your life. Thank you, Mom. I am forever grateful that I was blessed to have you as my mom.

To my son, Adam Pitchie. There is no other person or experience that fills my heart with such love and gratitude as I feel to be your mom. You are my greatest gift and miracle. Your Hebrew name, Nissan Chiam, which translates to "the miracle of life," represents everything I now believe in. It is because of you that my first book was named. It is because of you that The Miraculous Living Institute was birthed. It is because of you that my life has greater meaning. I am so proud of the man you are and continue to become. I love you, Adam.

To my Beloved, John Anella. To be gifted with such a rare and special love, especially at our age, is beyond a miracle and a blessing. Sharing life with you makes life much richer and sweeter. To be loved by you is a gift I never take for granted. I am beyond grateful that you found me, and now, we get to walk our remaining days together. Your love and support mean the world to me. And I look forward to all the wonderful adventures we will continue to create. I love you with all my heart.

And, to you, the reader. I am forever grateful that you have chosen to take this journey of creating a miraculous life with me. May these pages fill you with hope and inspiration and provide you with information and direction, so all your deepest desires come true. I wrote this book for you.

Love for *Create Your Miraculous Life*

Create Your Miraculous Life was written during very challenging times: a global pandemic, political and social unrest, to name a few. Yet, Wendy dug deep and shares ways to best support you, regardless of your circumstances. Everyone needs and will benefit from this information of purpose, passion and performance. You can now make living a miraculous life happen for you!

~Stedman Graham
New York Times Bestselling Author, Speaker,
Entrepreneur

Do you believe in miracles? Do you believe you can live a miraculous life? Wendy Darling has cracked the code and is going to show you how you can turn your deepest desires into a reality. As she says: If you have a desire in your heart...it's your truth.

~Cheryl D. Snapp Conner
Founder and CEO, SnappConner PR

Create Your Miraculous Life - It's NEVER Too Late will not only inspire you, you will be guided to the steps to take to fully awaken your deepest desires and finally learn how to materialize them. Those desires are yours. And they are there waiting for you to open your arms to receive them.

~September Dohrmann
CEO, CEO Space International

As human beings, we have two choices how we respond to the inexorable march of time: 1. We can live in fear that our time is running out or 2. We can act with the knowledge that it's never too late to be, do and have the important things in life. In this inspiring and powerful book (which is a quick and entertaining read), Wendy Darling teaches perspectives and techniques for creating an increasingly miraculous life - no matter how long you have been on this planet. This is, quite literally, wisdom for the ages.

~Steve Farber
Founder, The Extreme Leadership Institute
Author, *Radical Leap, Greater Than Yourself*
and *Love Is Just Damn Good Business*

The sign of a master is that they live what they facilitate in others. The sign of a masterful author is that they convey a lifetime's worth of wisdom in an incredibly easy-to-read way. The sign of a masterful trainer is that they translate their wisdom into easy-to-implement processes that invoke miraculous shifts. Wendy Darling embodies all of these things in this book. Give yourself the gift of allowing it to guide you toward creating a miraculous life. It truly is never too late.

~Dr. David Gruder
Integrative Psychologist
and 12-Awardwinning Bestselling Author

There is no better time than now to take a closer look at what matters to you most and finally have those dreams and desires materialize. Wendy Darling is going to take you on a journey to show you how you can, in fact, live a miraculous life.

~David M. Corbin
Two-time WSJ Bestselling Author, *Illuminate* and
Preventing BrandSlaughter

Living a miraculous life is your truth and destiny. Filled with stories and exercises, Wendy Darling guides you through the steps, regardless of your age or circumstances. Open your heart, your arms and receive all your desires waiting for you. Your time is now!

~Esther Wildenberg
Co-Founder and President, Bankcode Technologies

I love this book. Reading *Create Your Miraculous Life* was filled with so much value, I am surprised it all came from one book. I love Chapter 7 's exercise, "Creating My Future". Chapter 14 revealed even more about leaving my legacy, and I can't wait to begin using my "Miraculous Money Chart" from Chapter 15. Great stories. Great exercises. Great book!!!

~Mark Hattas
Executive, Entrepreneur, Author, and Coach

Create Your Miraculous Life - It's Never Too Late helps people realize that everyone's life is a miracle... that we were all born to live miraculous lives. Read this book!

~Paula Fellingham
Founder, Women's Information Network

The wisdom Wendy shares in her book touched me deeply. She has a beautiful way of inviting you in to consider and observe what could be different and ask what you truly desire in your life now. The deep wisdom she guides you through is profound.

~Ronita Godsi
iDezzine Consulting

Create Your Miraculous Life — It's NEVER Too Late

Mind blown - it's official. Thanks to Wendy Darling, *Create Your Miraculous Life – It's Never Too Late*, positively shifted my life. I quickly learned, through reading this entire book (which was a fantastic read) that there are really wonderful ways to help others that you love and at the same time, loving and helping yourself by figuring out what you need. Without one, the other will not be as enriching nor rewarding for anyone involved. Then, you can truly begin living a miraculous life. Wow, I mean really wow. Thank you, Wendy Darling!!

~Erin Saxton
www.TheErinNetwork.com

Table of Contents

Foreword

It has been said that a miracle can be a mere change in consciousness and that has certainly been my experience. Small changes are the unsung hero of a better life.

When I met Wendy, I was in awe of this soft-spoken, elegant woman's power. She saw me, I sensed, in a way that many others could not. Her words and questions were insightful and filled with childlike curiosity. I was hooked and wanted to know more about her. Doing work in the field of human potential put me in proximity to "thought-leaders" of all kinds, but Wendy Darling was something unique and special.

It was November 2017 and I was mid-pivot in a brand-new business. Things were good but perhaps not great. I was still living with a great deal of uncertainty and admittedly some fear about the road ahead. Sound familiar? Having crossed paths a few times, "Wendella" as I sometimes call her, offered me the gift of one of her audio meditations and some brain training cards.

The following are the original statements given to me by Wendy to facilitate some shifts in my consciousness (the "miracle"):

I AM FREE
IT IS SAFE TO BE ME
IT IS SAFE TO RECEIVE
I TRUST LIFE HAS MY BACK

I practiced and repeated these statements to myself and out loud. To say that they contributed to my wellbeing in all areas (including financially) is an understatement of some magnitude. They literally were miraculous.

When Wendy let me know that she was committed to sharing her insights and techniques through this book I was more than thrilled – for all of you!

"Create Your Miraculous Life."

Does that seem like a pretty tall order?

The fact that you are reading my words, right now, says that there is something within you that hopes, prays, even knows that you are destined to be living a rich, fulfilling and, yes, a miraculous life.

And, as Wendy expresses, it is NEVER too late to turn those desires of yours into reality.

This book was written during a global pandemic. Wendy's son also faced a health crisis. Her life was not feeling miraculous, at all. Yet there was an inner pull that she knew this topic was important, possibly even critical, during this period of time.

And like many things Wendy has taken on, she dug deep and allowed herself to find the place within her to once again experience the miracles life always has to offer. And, of course, to now be able to share this with you.

This book has been written to provide you with hope, inspiration and ideas of how you can be living a more miraculous life.

ANYTHING that you desire is your truth. What you want, wants you. And Wendy will show you how that can become available to you now.

Wendy Darling has cracked the code, mastering what you can do to finally create a miraculous life. There is great wisdom in what she shares, yet she makes your journey simple and easy to implement.

And it's not just the words on these pages that will have an impact on you. This book is infused with a lot of love. It is also infused with an energy that will assist you to shed your hurts, your heartaches, your trials and tribulations, and anything else that is interfering in you living a miraculous life. Allow yourself to breath it all in, nourishing each and every one of your cells.

You are capable of amazing things.

I have experienced the gifts Wendy Darling is able to provide. Her intuition and healing gifts are truly miraculous. This woman has a heart of gold and will do anything and everything to ensure your greatest success, for you to be living a miraculous life, materializing and fulfilling your deepest desires.

I'm grateful you have been led to pick up this book. I believe there is magic in these pages. Wendy has been able to crack the code to manifesting your deepest desires, while still fulfilling your life's purpose, what Wendy refers to as your Divine Destiny.

We at More Love Media know the power of love. We know miracles are not only possible, they are always available to you, each and every day. Love is the 'magic pill' that will open the floodgates for your personal and professional life.

Breathe deeply and take in the words Wendy offers. There is love and healing provided for you within each and every page.

Adam Markel

Speaker, Author of *Pivot, Change Proof,*
The I Love My Life Challenge

Chapter 1

My Miraculous Life

*"You can have nothing, you can come from nothing,
and still become everything you dream.
It's never too late."*

~ Oprah Winfrey

At the time of writing this book, I am 69 years of age. Although that could be seen as a fairly impressive number, my mind is in awe that so many years have already passed. Yes, I am forever grateful that I am still healthy and able to live an awesome life. I am also aware that there are probably fewer steps in front of me than are behind me.

That said, there are still so many more things I want to experience and products I want to produce, working with and influencing many more individuals to live rich, empowered lives. And, yes, to experience a miraculous life.

An interesting perspective from a 69-year-old?

Many people of my age have already retired. And for them, that's exactly what they want to be doing. Many people my age are not in a position to retire. And many, like me, are simply not interested.

But that is part of the gift I hope to be sharing with you. I hope, no matter what your circumstances may be, whatever your age is, that you realize it truly is never too late for you to experience anything you deeply desire in your life. Whether that be attracting the love of your life, starting a new career, beginning or growing your own business, improving your health or your wealth, or simply traveling around the world having amazing adventures—whatever it may be—it's never too late!

When I first began writing this book, I was focused entirely on the "It's Never Too Late" theme. However, I realized it's not only important that you recognize that it's never too late, but I also want you to realize that your life is a miracle. You were born to live a miraculous life.

I find it very interesting that, somehow, I got myself into the "miracle" business. My life certainly did not start that way. However, as I was creating my first book, *The Miracle That Is Your Life,* I began leaning more into this.

This all started when my wonderful publisher and best friend, Robbin Simons of Crescendo Publishing, and I were generating ideas for the chapters and title for my first book. Robbin's process is brilliant. She has a way of pulling out what you want to say and then helps to organize it all. We had sheets of paper and Post-it Notes all over the room. We had identified the chapters. And when she asked me what I thought the title of the book was, I found myself telling her the story of my son Adam's "baby naming."

In Judaism, when a child is born, he or she is given a Hebrew name. And typically, the child is given a name from a deceased member of your family. My father had recently passed away at the young age of 56 from a heart attack, so I knew I wanted to honor him.

His Hebrew name had been "Nissan," which translates to "miracle." So, I knew I wanted to give Adam my father's Hebrew name, Nissan.

My former husband's grandfather had also recently passed away, and we decided to honor him as well. His name was Charles. The Rabbi informed me that the Hebrew word for Charles is "Chaim," which translates to "life." So, my son's Hebrew name would be Nissan Chaim, which translates to *The Miracle of Life.*

I still remember how in awe I was of his name. Everything about being pregnant was miraculous to me. Holding my son for the very first time was beyond miraculous. Even though I knew, technically, how he became a person, my mind was in awe of this miracle baby. And even though my miracle baby is now 35 and a whopping 6'4", there is never a day that I am not grateful for the gift I was given to bring him into the world and be his mom.

And it was around the time of writing my first book that I felt led to rename and birth my new business name: The Miraculous Living Institute.

I certainly never imagined that I would put myself in the "miracle" business, but there has been something so very special about this. First, I love how this honors my father. Second, it reminds me of the most amazing gift of being Adam's mom. And third, it keeps me present to the miracles life offers each and every day.

Tapping into living a miraculous life was my personal learning curve, one that I hope to share with you in this book.

However, when I began writing this book, my life was not feeling miraculous in many ways. I had gone through an unusual period of time. I had lost my love, my passion, and my inspiration for my work. I also began struggling with my weight.

I wanted to feel inspired again. I wanted to feel more energetic again. I was not willing to put something on a piece of paper, my yearly goals and intentions, just to put something on a piece of paper.

And then, I had this thought: *The name of my business is The Miraculous Living Institute.* Here I was in the miracle business, and my life was not feeling miraculous...at all.

I find it very important to be living with integrity in all areas of my life. And I was feeling concerned that I was lacking integrity in living a miraculous life. It looked like I created yet another opportunity to learn and grow. And, of course, pass it on, paying it forward.

So, I knew what was going to be my year's theme and intention: living a miraculous life: creating miracles in all areas of my life.

In that moment, it felt like that was a very tall order and a far reach.

But I knew that was what I needed to focus on.

And, as it turned out, it truly was a stretch. But it also felt like Divine timing. I have written this book during a global pandemic, as well as a turbulent presidential election, the "Me Too" movement, and racial unrest, just to name a few. Personally, my son faced a significant health challenge that took up much of my time and attention. And a very close friend passed away.

So, if there was ever a better time to stretch and begin to create and experience miracles, it was now.

Somehow, I always seem to manage to get myself into these kinds of predicaments. However, if I cracked this nut, and this book is in print...well, I did it, and it was well worth it.

To me, miracles are doing something, experiencing something that you have resisted or simply have not been able to do or experience and are finally able to move forward. It's the unexpected. It's *finally* taking that walk, making that call—whatever steps you want to take, but simply have previously not been able to take them. And, of course, the *best* ones are those unexpected surprises that show up what seems like "out of nowhere" that delights us even more, lifts our spirits. A new opportunity. It's the surprise of money from an unexpected source. A new speaking engagement or client. Just yesterday, I received a call "out of nowhere" asking me to speak at their conference. The person in charge had "just happened" to find information about me. No direct referral.

It's these kinds of moments I live for. For me, it affirms how the heavens are continually conspiring to make all your wishes and deepest desires come true.

So, whatever those miracles might be for you, they are something to focus on, be delighted about, and open your heart and arms to welcome.

And the best part of beginning to acknowledge and appreciate those miraculous experiences and steps is that you open the door for more and even greater miracles to show up.

You will see me refer to this concept over and over again: *Whatever you desire, it is your truth.*

I know you might be thinking: "Wendy, you do not know my life or circumstances. Yes, I want to be making more money, I want to be having more fun—and is having a loving, intimate relationship really possible at this time of my life?"

You could probably make a long list of questions you keep asking yourself. I have probably asked many of those questions at different times in my life as well. Those inner discussions can make you feel horrible. And, unfortunately, that inner dialogue can continue to push your deepest desires away.

I *know* what it's like to keep trying to "make" life work. I know what it's like to feel empty and lonely. I know what it's like to work on making a living and attempting to grow a business. I know what it's like to run out of steam, wondering if my dreams were ever going to come true. I cannot even imagine how much ice cream, dark chocolate, and boxes of Kleenex I've used throughout the years.

And I also know what it's like to take a breath and somehow begin believing again.

Even though I've experienced many struggles, challenges, and heartaches, for some reason, I never gave up. I may have taken some time out to feel sorry for myself and lick my wounds (and, at times, more than just a little time out). But, eventually, I would dust myself off and rejoin the world and make another attempt at my life.

I also know what it's like to find it harder to dust myself off each time I had to attempt to bring myself out of the slump, the disappointment, the empty checking account, the broken heart—whatever the circumstances—to lift myself up.

But I also knew that it's not okay to give up...*ever.*

Even when you wonder if it's even possible for life to finally turn around and get better, easier. Even when you have no idea what you need to do differently. Especially when you want to give up.

So, if this possibly resembles anything close to how you are feeling, this book is for you no matter what your age and circumstances.

I want you to know that I'm here for you. I am challenging you to realize that *it's never too late.* And I want you to begin realizing that you are truly destined to live a miraculous life. I want you to know, in every fiber of your being, that *you* are a miracle. You were designed to be this amazing person, with special gifts, talents, and skills that no other person on this planet has to offer. That you and only you can make your special contribution. And we're going to take this journey together so you can finally breathe a little easier, enjoy life a little more, and flourish in this wonderful, miraculous life that is your Divine right—what I refer to as your Divine Destiny.

Your soul is crying out for you to dig deep, reach out,

and live. The Universe is here to show you the way. There are people wanting and waiting to meet you. And there is still so much you can offer to those who will most benefit from the gifts and talents that you and only you can provide.

As I look back at my own life, I am in awe of the accomplishments, the hurdles, and the experiences I have already had. I have loved, been loved, and had the privilege of being a mom to my amazing son. I inherited a wonderful stepson, his wife, and my two grandsons. I have been blessed with extraordinary friends and family.

Yet my life was not always a "cakewalk." In fact, it started off rather challenging.

I grew up in a home where I had a good relationship with my father. However, he traveled a lot with business. My mother was a very strict parent and was also mentally, emotionally, and physically abusive. For many years, I had no idea that life could be any other way. I learned very quickly to "read" her moods and stay out of her way.

Because it was so important for her to literally rule our home, I never had the opportunity to discover who I was and find my own way of doing things. It was always doing things her way. And whatever I did, it was usually met with not doing it "quite right." As a young adult, this left me searching for guidance and approval outside of myself. So, my safety, level of happiness, and satisfaction were based on my outside circumstances and world.

However, once I left home to go to college, I began to excel in school. I finally was not under my mom's pressure, and I guess I was breathing easier for the first time in my life.

And then I excelled in my career. I started out as a sixth-grade teacher for a year, then returned to school to obtain two graduate degrees.

I had an awesome opportunity to be Dean of Students for Semester at Sea right out of graduate school, responsible for 700+ co-educational students while we sailed around the world. I could write a whole book just from those 4 months alone.

Dean of Students, at that time, was my long-term goal. So, when I returned, I was not sure what I was going to do.

The Training and Development industry was in its infancy at that time, and I had the opportunity of being a part of the Training and Development arm for the State of Missouri. We provided consulting, training, and development to all 15 state departments. My experiences were rich and paved the way for starting my own business in 1981.

Meanwhile, I had married and had my son, Adam. My father had also suddenly passed away at the young age of 56, which left me devastated. He was my rock, and after he left, my world didn't feel as safe. And this is when life started to get a little wobbly.

I was *so* happy being a mom. And I loved my consulting work. However, I got a little too involved in work and a little too distracted by the attention of the men I was working with. I eventually succumbed to temptation and was unfaithful to my husband.

I must admit, there are very few things I completely regret in the choices I have made, but this is one that still has a tender spot within me. I handled myself so inappropriately and hurt the one person who I was to cherish and make his world a safe and beautiful place.

Understandably, he was deeply hurt.

I confessed to him the evening before I was to leave for a consulting job in LA. I was really sick at that time, but I was a "Type A," workaholic kind of person, so it was not even an option that I not go.

I barely slept that evening. It was horrible.

The next day, I was at the Dallas-Ft. Worth airport preparing to fly to LA. I had been sick to my stomach, so I decided to go outside and get some fresh air before leaving on my flight. Unfortunately, I passed out, fell over a ledge, and fell approximately 25 feet.

I was taken to the hospital where, at first, they didn't know if my shattered right leg could be saved. I had multiple surgeries over several months to rebuild my leg, not knowing if I would ever walk again. The good news is that after 11 months, I was able to begin walking.

I also suffered multiple back fractures.

I was much later diagnosed with a traumatic brain injury that took years to recover from. Although I still have some minor issues, I am blessed to the extent I was able to recover.

That said, my accident was nothing compared to what was going to happen next.

Around the fourth week in the hospital, my husband came with suitcases packed, saying he no longer wanted to be married. We obviously had been having problems, but my confession had sealed the deal.

When we eventually went to court to finalize our

divorce, he was awarded full custody of our son, who was only 4.5 at the time. This is when I literally broke into many pieces.

My body and life were simply a reflection of how broken I literally was. And my journey was about picking up the pieces, one by one, seeing where I had gotten so off-track to have all of this happen and what choices I was now going to make to dig myself out of this hole.

And it has been quite a journey.

It's hard to believe that my accident was already 30 years ago, and it's been a 30-year journey of discovering who I am, what is special about me, what kind of work I can offer, and where I can make a difference. I was starting at ground zero.

But I never gave up.

This is also when I began to open up and receive my healing gifts and what has become my transformational results system: The Miraculous Living Method.

Prior to my accident, I knew nothing about healing, energy, etc. But little by little, I was having insights, awareness, and even singing that began coming out of me and helping me heal. Of course, I began realizing that I now had the ability and opportunity to offer this to others, helping them with their personal and professional journeys.

I'm not going to lie: It took quite a while to "come out of the closet" with all of this. But I eventually realized that I had been given a very special gift. And gifts are meant to be shared. So, I got over myself and began working with others. First, me. Then, my friends. Then, I started to offer this to my clients. And they were getting amazing results. I feel deeply honored and proud I can contribute this way.

I had suffered for so long. I didn't want anyone else to suffer. And I was given a gift to free people from their past and begin living the life of their dreams. Truly miraculous and so very special.

So, little by little, I was finding my way.

Little by little, I was discovering how to create and experience the miracles and magic of life.

And, little by little, I was living the life of *my* dreams.

And this is what I want for you.

Let's continue.

Dear God:

Deep within me, I believe you are here for me, wanting me to have everything I've desired. I know that it's getting harder to believe. Please fill me with your love, help me feel you within me and my life. Help me believe and know that there is something better, more special trying to come into my life. Fill me with hope and faith. I truly don't want to feel this way, but I'm not sure what has me in this state of mind and heart. Thank you for loving me, for guiding me, and always having my back.

Chapter 2

It's NEVER Too Late

As I write these words, I am rapidly approaching my 70th birthday. I'm not going to lie; that just seems a bit twisty in my mind, but my mind is simply going to have to adjust.

There is so much more I want to experience. So much more I want to accomplish. So much more that I want to do. And, fortunately, this theme of "It's Never Too Late" is alive and well within me. It gives me hope, drive, and inspiration. Even though I have many years behind me, I also know I still have opportunity (and hopefully time) to experience more.

And I have my mom to thank for gifting me this lesson. In fact, as I write this, today is my mom's 92nd birthday.

And since we are in the midst of COVID-19, my sisters and I were blessed to be able to have a Zoom birthday party with her, which was really nice. Thank goodness for technology.

I already have mentioned that my mom was really hard on me growing up. Yet, in her mid-40s, my mom ended up seeing a therapist and began making significant changes. She then went back to college and finished her undergraduate work as well as her master's when she was in her late 40s. She then started a career in social work in her 50s. So, my mom taught me "it's never too late" to heal, grow, and change. She also taught me "it's never too late" to begin a new career.

Then, she taught me another valuable lesson: It's never too late for love.

A couple of years after my father passed away, my mom began dating. My sisters and I were really impressed that she was meeting many good men. And after a couple of years, she met Ted, whom she later married. They had an amazing relationship and were married just shy of 21 years when Ted passed away.

Even after Ted passed away, my mom welcomed love for a third time at age 82. However, her health began declining from dementia, and we eventually found it necessary to place her in assisted living and she is now in a wonderful memory care facility (about 10 minutes from where I live).

I feel her lessons have been powerful. Some of her lessons were tough. She taught me how I didn't want to be. Because of the contrast, I was able to be a more loving, accepting, and generous person. I was a very different mother with my son. And because of my father's unconditional love and encouragement, he left me with the lesson of never giving up and going for my dreams. Because he died at such an early age, he also taught me that there are no guarantees in life and to live fully. I feel what I do today honors my father and the life he gave to me. In more recent years, I was also able to transform the relationship with my mom.

And, fortunately, giving up was not my strong suit—although the challenges were beginning to wear me down.

So, this book is going to be about what I have learned. By the end of this book, I am going to show you how to reach for the stars, turn your life around, and have your heart's desires fulfilled.

I believe with every fiber of my being that the desires of your heart were put there to remind you of who you *really* are, what you are capable of experiencing, and having you stretch not only to reach your potential, but to make *your* mark in life. I believe we are all born with gifts that, when cultivated, have the ability to make a difference.

What still lives in your heart that you deeply desire to experience?

As I mentioned, we are in the midst of a global pandemic as I write this book. Never in our entire lives have we experienced anything like this. Between the virus, political unrest, rioting, jobs lost, and people clearly struggling, it doesn't take a rocket scientist to see we are struggling in so many ways.

I found myself wondering how we were going to come out of this situation. What is happening that so many people are unhappy, angry, and frustrated? As I write, I do not have any answers to that, yet. But I do feel it may get worse before it gets better. I hope I am wrong.

And the theme of "it's never too late" is now very timely, maybe even critical. Many need to feel more hope. More support. We are going to have to build our world from a renewed foundation.

It's never been more important for you to step up and step out. For you to offer whatever gifts and talents you have, to be a part of the healing our world needs.

Contributing your gifts and talents will make a difference that is very much needed today.

THIS IS YOUR TIME! There are people waiting and wanting what you have to offer—the gifts and talents that you and only you can provide. Whether it be supporting a good friend or having a service or product reaching those who can benefit, your life and contribution matters and makes a difference.

Allow me to act as your personal fairy godmother, as I share with you the lessons I have learned in my lifetime.

Let the games begin!

Dear God:

Deep within me, I know I still have more to offer. Help restore my faith, knowing I can and will have a better life. Help provide me with the courage and determination to take my next steps. Help me know that it's never too late. I thank you for all your love and support.

Chapter 3

Your Miraculous Opportunity

"There are only two ways to live your life.
One is as though nothing is a miracle.
The other is as though everything is a miracle."

~ Einstein

As mentioned, I'm writing during a forced time out in our world. We are experiencing COVID-19. Never in my lifetime have I experienced anything like this.

Yet, despite all these very legitimate concerns, I can't help but wonder how this possibly holds an opportunity. An opportunity of deciding what matters most. An opportunity to slow down. An opportunity to pull together as a family, as a community, as a nation, as a world.

It's a wake-up call like none other we've ever experienced.

What are you choosing? Even if you are reading this many months/years after this event, this is your opportunity to take a closer look at what matters most to you.

What do you want?

Could this be the opportunity to focus on what really matters and makes a difference in your life? Your health? Your relationships? How you contribute to the world? Isn't that what ultimately matters the most?

What might you be tired of dealing with? Where might you be struggling?

Maybe it's finally time to find the places within you that have been buried deep, keeping you from living a more fulfilling, miraculous life.

Let's continue.

Dear God:

Even though you know how much I want to feel the relief of experiencing life in a gentler, easier way, please help me release the internal thoughts and emotions that are fighting to keep that from happening. I can no longer fight. Help me find gentler, kinder, more loving ways to accept myself. Love myself. Appreciate myself. Help me recognize the beauty life has to offer. Help me find the next step that will take me in a healthier and happier direction. Help me discover the magic that truly exists in our world today.

Chapter 4

How Miracles Are Birthed: Creating a Miraculous Life

We have hopefully established that if there is anything that you truly desire to experience in your life, it's never too late. Anything is possible, especially if it's in alignment with your purpose in life.

Oops. A bit of a loophole.

You need to create your vision and mission. You need to identify your purpose, the "why," so you are best positioned for ultimate success.

You need to create a container to allow this all to take form in your life. This is how you begin going from a desire to an idea, to actually turning it into reality.

But before we go any further, I want to explain how the role of working with "energy" will make all the difference in what you can produce.

Most of us have learned that if we have a goal, our target, and next steps, ultimately we have a pretty good chance of accomplishing that. For example, you decide you want to lose 15 pounds. So, you decide how you want to eat differently and also start getting more exercise.

And so you begin.

However, after a few days, you discover you didn't follow your eating plan. And you didn't get your planned exercise in.

The same is true for a work idea. You had this great idea, took a couple of steps, but then something happened. You realize you stopped moving forward. In fact, you even may have forgotten you wanted to do this.

This is where it gets interesting.

For many years, I used my process to look for thoughts and beliefs that were limiting my actions and results. However, after learning more about how the mind works, I realized that I had inadvertently programmed myself to always be looking for what was wrong and not working. That meant I was living in a "find it and fix it" mentality, which continues to strengthen the neural pathway and belief that "something is always wrong."

Then, one amazing day, I had the thought: What if I was examining from an incorrect perspective? What if we had it backward? Instead of looking to the past, what if we created our future and, in doing so, could it still be possible the past can be released?

So, I experimented.

The Miraculous Living Method is (partially) comprised of Sound Healing, Hands-On Transformational Energy Cards, and Affirming Statements and Scenarios.

The sound healing carries the energetic frequency of love. By itself, it is very effective. After my transformational cards were birthed, I started to combine them with the sound healing. Now the process became even more effective.

Because of what I have learned about the "frequency of energy," the feelings of love and gratitude actually carry a higher vibration, which allows the feelings with a lower vibration, such as anger and sadness, worry, and frustration to be melted and loved away. The sound healing carries this higher frequency as do the transformational cards. While listening to the sound healing and placing your hands on the transformational cards, they create a unique and effective energy "loop".

Then, I added "affirmations" to the mix. When you say an affirmation in the bubble of the sound healing and transformational cards, old and erroneous thoughts rise to the surface and can be released (actually, the emotional charge associated with the thought and/or feeling). Meanwhile, the mind begins to strengthen whatever thought is being infused. This is either strengthening an existing neural pathway, or—if one does not already exist—the process creates a new one. Now, your energetic vibration increases. You now are in energetic alignment with your desired goal.

But it doesn't stop there.

Taking this approach, the Miraculous Living Method provides the vehicle for even better results. Life becomes easier, more peaceful. Taking action becomes easier. Results are achieved faster.

So, it is not *just* the physical that needs our attention. We must focus on your Energy System, Your Mind/Body/Emotional/Spiritual system.

That is how you create a miraculous life!

There is obviously a lot more to what I'm talking

about, but I will be sprinkling ideas that you can begin incorporating into your life now!

Dear God,

I am beyond grateful to be learning how to be more connected with you. To be able to tap into your infinite wisdom that you are continuously pouring through me. That your Divine Loving Energy helps me to release the blocks that have been keeping away all the good you've been trying to provide for me. I am grateful that I am learning how to love and release those places of stuck energy and emotions. I am grateful I am learning how to support my mind to be thinking healthier and happier thoughts. I am forever grateful that I am on this incredible journey of creating a miraculous life.

Chapter 5

What Takes You to Your Knees Gives You Strength to Rise

The time after my accident was the most challenging time in my life. The trauma of my accident left me fearful and vulnerable, two emotions I had never really experienced in my adult life. I had previously been a person who never thought twice about taking a risk, entering new territory. Now, I had immediately become someone who did not trust herself or anything else about life. Not a fun place to live. The reality was, those insecurities had always been there. They were just buried alive and now revealed.

I discovered that I had been living my life on a shaky

foundation and significantly overcompensating from the wounds of my childhood.

At the beginning of my recovery, I was wondering and primarily focused on what it was going to take to heal my body. My leg had been shattered, and for many months, I had a lot of uncertainty if I would be able to walk again. I also had a broken back, so I was (obviously) not in a very active stage of my life. Between surgeries (I had five of them to repair my leg), I would do what I could to rebuild my strength. I would walk as far as I could on crutches. I remember the first time I tried, I was able to walk as far as the end of my driveway. Eventually, I walked throughout my neighborhood. People would stop and cheer me on. Many said that when they saw me "walking," they felt there was no excuse for them.

Those moments meant the world to me, since I could not see how my future was going to unfold. It was a very confusing and soul-searching time for me.

Mainly, I felt tremendous pain in my heart.

And around the time I began getting stronger, the biggest blow was about to happen.

When my former husband and I eventually went to court, the judge awarded full custody of our son to him.

Losing custody of my son literally finished me off. The best way I can explain what happened to me was it felt like something "snapped" inside my brain. It was like a critical "connector" in my life's circuitry broke.

I'm sharing my story because I believe we all have things in our life that potentially take us to our knees. We all have made choices whose consequences provided us with a wake-up call of what is most important, and what needs to change.

Maybe that time for you is now?

If you are reading this, I can almost state with complete certainty that your life has taken you down to *your* knees, in your own unique way. You aren't sure how you can possibly get up. Hopefully it has not been as extreme as my circumstances. You may be running out of steam. You may be wondering if a better quality of life is possible. You are possibly wondering if you have used up your "jump starts" and the opportunities in your life.

Well, I'm here to say...You have not missed your opportunities.

It's just going to take a little tweaking for you to fill yourself back up with a whole lot of hope and a deep sense that you are going to turn your desires into reality...now.

It's never too late. And it's never too late to create and live a miraculous life.

So, let's keep going with this conversation between us.

Dear God:

I come to you with a heavy heart. I keep trying to stay optimistic, but it sometimes feels impossible. I know there is a better life waiting for me, but I am tired of the "trying." Please help me. Be with me. Find ways to encourage me. Help restore my faith. Help to release this pain that still exists in my heart. Help me know I have the opportunity for a better today, and an even better tomorrow.

Chapter 6
What's It Going to Take?

How many times have you asked that question?

Are you one of those people who has been dedicated to your life? You've been responsible, attempting to do the right things. Maybe you have immersed yourself in personal growth work, but you haven't seen the payoffs.

Or maybe, like many who come into my community, you are just worn out from doing everything you "thought" you should do, and now, you just feel tired and empty.

You may have money in your bank, but your "love bank" is empty. You may have climbed the corporate ladder, but you've been sleeping alone for way too long.

Or maybe you know it's time for a change, and you are not certain what that may be.

You may have thought you were doing all the "right" things but are suddenly shocked when your spouse announces they don't love you anymore and wants a divorce.

Maybe a significant life event happened that put your job at risk or made you unable to work. Maybe you ran out of money, finding yourself knee-deep in debt.

I think I could list many examples.

Yet, you are reading this book, so I know you have not given up. You really do believe that there is a better life still available for you. Thank goodness.

I *know* that there is a Universal intelligence that is looking out for you, guiding you in ways to fulfill your deepest desires. I believe these "forces" have been with you your entire life. In fact, I actually believe your desires are placed within you so that you grow, develop, and contribute in a way you were designed to live and contribute.

I am a spiritual person, so please choose what words may serve you most. I believe in God. I welcome and embrace all religions. I also believe we have a "team" of guides that are assigned to keep a closer eye on us. I believe your soul speaks to you through the desires of your heart. And this guidance, when cultivated, is just about all you need to experience and accomplish everything you could ever desire in your life. Talk about having an executive coach! God, your soul, and your "team" is the best there is.

Yet, if this is true, what has happened that most people don't even know they can live this way? If you are one of those people, your life is about to get a whole lot better.

I'll speak from my own experience first.

As I already stated, I was never really encouraged to think for myself. I was a sensitive girl and could feel things most people could not. It served me well, since I could sense when my mom was in one of her moods and when it was best to avoid being anywhere near her.

Because I was told what to think, feel, and do, I did not know myself. How can you trust something you don't even know? That's not a very great position to be in, given all the choices and actions that are necessary to navigate through life.

Confidence in myself was lacking. Yes, I did some very smart things to build more confidence in myself, but after my accident, I discovered I had built my "house" on a very shaky foundation. All the years during my recovery meant peeling back the layers of hurt and protection and allowing the real me to peek my way through.

This became a dance. For a while, I would begin feeling more confident and able to take action. I was also able to be more authentically me. And because this was new, like having new skin, I could easily feel more *tender*. It didn't take much for this girl to poke her head back into her shell.

And maybe I'm not alone.

In working with thousands of people, I think we all feel a little naked as we walk into new territory.

So, let's keep moving forward so you can create a life that you are totally and completely in love with.

Dear God:

I want to believe. I want to believe that you are here for me, wanting me to thrive in my life. I want to believe that there is a better life for me. I'm tired. I'm tired of trying. I'm tired of hoping, wishing, and dreaming. I'm really running out of steam. Help fill me with your love. Help fill me with a renewed sense of hope. Help me believe, once again, that it's not too late, that my dreams can come true now. Thank you for not losing sight of me and continuing to encourage me to take one more step.

Chapter 7

What Do You Want to Experience?

This is the part of your journey to get deeply honest about what you want to experience in life. Maybe it's finally welcoming love into your life. Maybe it's exploring a new career or business. Maybe it's strengthening your finances and creating wealth. Maybe it's regaining your health. Learning how to paint. Or simply finding new ways to have fun. Maybe it's all of these and *more*. Only you know what it is that you want.

You have the opportunity and responsibility to identify your life's purpose, your mission in life.

I also believe that there are *many* different ways to do that.

My purpose is assisting people to fulfill their purpose, their Divine Destiny, while living the life of their dreams.

For me, having my dreams fulfilled is telling me I am "on track" to fulfilling my Divine Destiny.

I don't believe that you have to fulfill your purpose first. In fact, I believe that some of your dreams coming true are simply confirmation that you are on the right path.

For example, I have always wanted a home either by the ocean, or at least be positioned so that I *see* the ocean from my backyard.

For many years I lived in Texas, so that was pretty far away from an ocean. But now I live about two miles from the ocean. I don't yet have that house with the view, but I'm sure a lot closer to my ultimate dream home than I was before.

I have had too many clients who have experienced success, but their personal lives aren't so great. Or some who were challenged with their career. I help them discover what they truly want to experience.

We typically discover a deep desire that has not yet materialized. And once identified, they begin giving themselves permission to feel and open their hearts to allow that to happen.

You will begin to feel greater happiness, more success, and more fulfillment. And this is before your desire is even materialized. I have experienced this for myself, as well as with my clients, that when you begin to give yourself permission to welcome "whatever that desire is" into your life, life starts to feel better and there tends to be more movement.

Let's compare your desire to a beachball. A beachball is very light. However, when you hold a beachball under water, it takes a certain amount of effort to keep it there.

Your buried desire is similar. It takes energy to keep a desire buried. But once you embrace that desire, it's just like releasing the beachball and allowing it to pop out of the water.

You'll find you begin to feel lighter, better. You'll notice feeling more hopeful. And you also begin to have "synchronistic" experiences. There is also the possibility that you may have some underlying issues show up; however, you may be more aware that this needs to be dealt with (the gift of the Miraculous Living Method).

Let's take a little time for you to get honest about what you truly desire.

Exercise: Magic Wand Time. Take out your journal or a piece of paper. Place your hands over your heart, taking a few deep breaths. If it helps, play some relaxing music (or a Miraculous Living Method audio).

You are going to take the time to create the life of your dreams. Just answer the following questions. Let your heart speak through your pen. This is not an exercise to think. This is an exercise to feel. Don't be concerned if this can happen or how it can happen. Simply give yourself permission to bring your dreams and desires back to life. Wave your magic wand, and live the life of your desires:

Where are you living?

Who are you living with?

What does your home look like?

Describe your health.

Who are the most important people in your life? Your family? Friends? How do you connect and spend time together?

Do you have a career? What are you doing? How are you contributing?

Describe your finances. Your savings/investments/assets?

Describe your spirituality. What does that mean for you? What effect does that have on the way you live your life?

Next, write out a scenario, a description, of your future life. This is describing the life you are living, as if it is true now. The saying goes, "if you can dream it, you can be it." Describe how you are sitting or walking through your dream home. Describe how it looks. Describe how it makes you feel. Continue to do this with the other areas. Now, you have a summary of your desired, miraculous life.

This is your life. This is your future. This can be your reality. If you truly created this from the core of your heart, I can say with confidence that this is your Life By Design.

Dear God:

I know that you want every single desire that lives in my heart to materialize. In fact, I believe you want even more for me than I want for myself. Help me believe again. Restore my hope. Help me regain my faith. Let me bask in your love. And from there, allow me to know the truth of who I am and all that I am to experience. And please guide me toward my next step so that I am one step closer to having my dreams fulfilled. Thank you for loving me, believing in me, and guiding me.

Chapter 8
Wendy, You're Crazy

For quite a while after my accident and losing custody of my son, I became very cautious and deliberate with my choices and the way I lived my life. I had been deeply traumatized, but I was also embarrassed and ashamed of what had happened.

I wanted to feel okay again, and I was trying very hard to get there. Maybe too hard.

But I finally reached a point where I began surrendering a bit more to life again. I no longer had the energy to fight, and that was probably the best thing that could have happened to me.

Early on, I had made the difficult decision to move to

Dallas, which was approximately 90 miles from where my son was living. It was terribly painful, but I was finding it challenging to earn a decent living in the town where we both lived.

Meanwhile, in those early weeks of living in Dallas, I was "pounding the pavement" attempting to find work. I was living with friends. One day, I simply looked at my friend and said, "I'm going to bed." And shortly after I began taking naps (something I have never really done most of my life), the phone began ringing. It was clear that I needed to rest and recover from all the trauma I had experienced.

I later attended one of my first personal growth retreats to help me continue my recovery and replenish myself.

At one point in the retreat, we were all dancing. One of the men, Glen, who was dancing next to me, looked at me and said, "Wendy, you're crazy!" And I remember looking back at him, smiling and saying, "I know!" And then he said, "No, I mean, you are really crazy!" And, once again, I smiled and said, "I know!"

What I hadn't shared before was that when my former husband and I were in court, his attorney tried to make my accident look like a suicide attempt (which was not true) and that I was "crazy" because I was opening up more to my spirituality.

How it was handled was extremely hurtful, especially since it was not true.

So, for a long time, I lived a very "narrow" life, doing my best to appear "normal."

When that man said those words to me while we were dancing, something just clicked—in a good way.

I remember sharing with the group what Glen had said to me. And for the first time in a long time, I felt *free*! I shared with the group that I *am* crazy! I'm crazy about life...I'm crazy about my son...I'm crazy about people!

And the reason I bring this up is that there may be parts of you that you have been hiding and are buried within you.

Are you holding yourself back in some ways, believing this will protect you and prevent you from being hurt again?

All too often when we have been hurt or have experienced a failure, there can be a tendency to hold ourselves back. It's understandable that you don't want to be hurt or disappointed, but it's also important to allow yourself to take risks, be willing to make a mistake, be hurt, or even fail. Moving forward in life has no guarantees. But not moving forward also has its costs, possibly creating unnecessary heartache and pain.

Be willing to put yourself out there again. Be willing to look silly or even crazy. Be willing to feel scared, uncertain, and vulnerable. Until you are willing to do any of that, things are not going to change.

The Universe loves it when we take *action*! And remember, any step is one step closer to fully living your miraculous life.

So, whatever happened, lick your wounds, dust yourself off, and get back on the horse of life again—whatever your "horse" actually is.

Need to find a job? Dust off your resume and start sending it out. Need to lose some weight? Start to drink a little more water, add more veggies to your day, and get a little movement (even if it's just a walk down the street).

Resistance is typically present when we are wanting something different but not really doing anything about it. Maybe you are making your "whatever" into too big of a bite. Chunk it down to tiny steps. And be willing to take just one of them.

And if you look at resistance as the part of you that

is attempting to keep you safe, maybe you can have a conversation with the resistance (see Chapter 19 - *My Favorite Miracle Making Practices*), showing that you are being responsible, taking good care of yourself, and just going to take a small step in the direction toward what you ultimately want to experience.

I have a client who I am working with right now. She's lovely. She's 69. And she has not had an intimate relationship with someone in almost 20 years. And yet, this is something that she deeply desires.

She is retired and can live almost anywhere she chooses. And for many years, she has wanted to move from where she currently lives. And even though she almost put her home on the market, something always seems to happen and she simply stops.

And this is where we began dealing with the resistance. The part of her that becomes immobilized at the thought of change, forcing her to find herself between a rock and a hard place.

She began loving the resistance, honoring the resistance, educating the part of her that was fearful of change. And soon, she had more freedom to actually make the move she'd wanted to make for many years. In fact, she very spontaneously bought a townhome close to where one of her sons and his family live. She amazed herself and even shocked her son, who never thought she would move. It happened easily, and rather magically. She even purchased it without seeing it in-person. This was a huge step for her. This demonstrated how much freer she was to now live the life of her desires.

So, I encourage you to continue to look at what you truly desire.

What story are you telling yourself, possibly keeping your desires away? How have you built walls, keeping yourself safe but also keeping you from turning your dreams and desires into reality?

Once you unlock that door, it will begin to feel like the waters have parted and you are in a beautiful flow of rich life experiences.

Dear God:

I am feeling the pull of my heart, wanting to experience much more in my life. I want to feel happier. I want to be contributing more. I no longer want to hide from life. Help me heal the parts of me that still feel unsafe in our world. Help me heal the parts of me that are afraid to be seen. Help me heal the parts of me that are afraid to express what I really feel, what I really think, and what I really know. Help me open up to receive all the goodness life has to offer.

Chapter 9

It's Never Too Late to Learn to Love Yourself

The first stop on the road to success begins with *you*.

Maybe you already know that. Perhaps you are the kind of person who gives to everyone who crosses your path, yet you neglect yourself. Over-giving to others can also be a convenient distraction.

Learning to love yourself is a lifelong practice. Just like any relationship, it takes time. It requires attention. And a whole lot of love and acceptance.

So, where to begin?

How about taking stock of how you currently treat yourself?

- HOW ARE YOU TREATING YOUR BODY? When you look in the mirror, do you look at yourself with love in your eyes, or do you immediately focus on your wrinkles or body parts that don't quite match up to how you would prefer to look? Do you nourish yourself with foods that best support your body, or do you eat whatever you can get your hands on? Do you get outside, get some movement, and strength train? Do you rest and get good quality sleep?

- WHAT DOES YOUR DAY LOOK LIKE? Are you grateful for what you experience, or do you find yourself complaining about your job and your responsibilities?

- HOW HAPPY ARE YOU? The degree you love yourself is directly correlated to the degree of happiness you can experience. Do you feel happy and satisfied with your life? Or do you find yourself complaining about some or all aspects of your life? (Are you even aware of when you may be complaining?) Do you feel connected to a higher power, knowing you are never really alone? Or do you feel disconnected and isolated from the world, not knowing where you fit or belong?

- WHAT ARE YOU MOST GRATEFUL FOR? How easy is it to feel gratitude for yourself? For your life?

I'm sure we could discover more, but this is a good place to start.

What's really wonderful is, the more you love yourself—and treat yourself with love, acceptance, kindness, even admiration—the more you open yourself up to magnetize and experience a richer life. More than likely, this is the life you currently desire.

So, even though loving yourself can be a more challenging piece of the equation to having your deepest desires fulfilled, it does not have to be hard.

Remember, this is a process, not a destination. So, you just need to begin practicing.

What might be some ways you can demonstrate acts of love toward yourself?

(For more ideas on how you can incorporate more love for yourself, see Chapter 19 - My Favorite Miracle Making Practices)

Learning to love yourself, value yourself, and appreciate yourself is one of the kindest gifts you can give to yourself. It makes the difference between living an "okay" life to being able to live a miraculous life.

If you have been challenged to create the life of your dreams, please take time each and every day to show yourself love. Provide yourself with acts of love. Only you can decide what those might be, but it will make a difference in your health, your wealth, and your overall sense of success and fulfillment.

Dear God:

I am blessed to have been given this opportunity of life. I also recognize that my life has provided me challenges that have allowed me to grow. I am learning to value myself and appreciate myself. Please provide me with the confidence of knowing how special I really am. I thank you for all you provide so that I truly can love myself and the life I have been given.

Chapter 10

It's Never Too Late for Optimal Health

As I write this, I am 69.5. I must admit, I find it hard to believe that so many years have already passed me by. And, even though I am relatively healthy, my body is beginning to show a bit more wear and tear.

Of all the obstacles I've had to overcome in my life, creating a healthy relationship with my body has been a challenge. Growing up, I was shy and insecure. Looking back, I realize it was easier to be upset with my body than dealing with my feelings of hurt and inadequacy.

Because my mom was so highly critical and abusive, I learned at a very early age that food would calm my system. It, unfortunately, became my best friend. It also later became my worst enemy.

My mom and sisters were underweight, whereas I had a slightly fuller, but very normal size. So, I also had a skewed image of what a normal body size looked like.

My body was an incredible partner at showing where I still needed to heal, where I needed to make some adjustments with my nourishment and movement.

These are the steps I've taken, which I also suggest to my clients:

1. *No more diets!* Take time to really learn to listen to your body. To begin, start by getting rid of any foods that may be taking away from your optimal health. Pay attention to how you feel after you eat something. I also believe in balance. I am not recommending anything specific for you. For example, I am typically on a 2 for 1 rotation: two days of lower carb, one day of a more balanced meal. This also seems to be helping "trick" my body, and it has increased my metabolism. Start logging your food, water, and exercise, weigh once a week. There are many apps available for that. Learn what your body wants and needs. Be sure not to restrict yourself; instead, learn to choose an occasional

treat and enjoy it, in moderation. I now experience *so* much more freedom. I hope you will too.

2. *Add healthier choices, as opposed to just taking foods away.* What that means is that, if you still have foods that you love, add something healthy to that meal on occasion. For example, you really want that slice of pizza. Go for it. And add a salad.

3. *Make the effort to drink more water.* This one strategy is a major contributor to your health. Add more vegetables and some fruit, making sure you get lots of fiber in your day. As you continue to eat a more nutritious, balanced way of eating, you will no longer—or very rarely—have any cravings. Don't you love that?

4. *Design your first steps.* I think one of the mistakes many make is having an "all or nothing approach." It might work for a while, but the more extreme you may be in one direction, the other extreme may boomerang right before your eyes.

I have had many times in my life where I have been healthy, lean, and fit. And it seems that when I need to do more healing work, my body tends to speak with me in the form of excess weight. Isn't that interesting? So, if excess weight is one of your issues, maybe there are "issues in your tissues" that are trying to get your attention.

If you think that having a healthy body is all about the food you eat, please think again. Yes, nutrition is important. But as I have said before, "the issues in your tissues are creating the junk in your trunk."

Love truly is the answer to a healthy body and life. It was the reason I created my program "Loving Yourself Lean." I wanted others to love themselves and their body more. And the natural result is releasing excess weight. I have also seen this to be true with clients who were experiencing other kinds of health issues.

So, becoming aware and learning about the connection between self-love, being healthy, and creating a healthy body is your path to living a miraculous, healthy life.

Begin appreciating all the gifts your body provides. A significant wake-up call was when my father passed away at the young age of 56 from a heart attack. I am very much like my father, so I had tests to make sure I was okay. When I had the tests, I got to see my heart in action! *Wow*! That was a moment that is etched in my memory. I was amazed at how hard, fast, and consistent it was (and is) working! Truly amazing what that sweetheart does each and every day. Talk about running a marathon!

And this provided me with even greater appreciation for how wonderful my body is and the importance of cherishing it.

This becomes increasingly more important as we age. It's not just about being at an optimal weight. It's doing whatever you can to be able to support your body, to make it easier for your body to do all the many functions that are needed each and every day.

I'm pretty sure you want to live a long and healthy life. I would imagine there is more of life you want to experience. Think of caring for your body like a newborn baby who is totally dependent on you taking care of it. You would never consider giving a newborn pizza, fries, and a beer. So, think about what your body really needs. Learn to honor your body. Cherish it for all it has done all these years to get you to where you are today.

How are you caring for "the temple of your soul?" What are you doing to nourish and support your body? And what can you begin to do to take better care of your body?

If you know you have neglected your health, it's never too late to make changes. The body has an amazing ability to recover! It wants to be healthy. All it needs is a little support from you.

Do what you can to demonstrate to your body how much you love, value, and appreciate it. Your body is longing for your love, for your support.

This interview is with my friend, David Corbin. When I first met David approximately 9 years ago, he mentioned he had recently lost a lot of weight. And 9 years later, he is still lean and healthy. Probably even more so.

David is a corporate consultant and speaker. He had been working hard, but life caught up with him. He found himself weighing 195 pounds on his 5'5" frame, which, he admits, is clinically obese. At the time, David was 59 years old.

David had divorced, so he started paying more attention to his appearance. However, it was a woman he was dating who opened his eyes. She questioned why he was never "alone." David felt he was alone a lot. However, he was alone watching TV, maybe reading a book. She suggested meditating. And that changed everything for David.

As David spent more time with himself, staying still, he was able to regroup with the "Divine." He found that as he became more mindful of himself, he also became more aware of his body. And that he described as "delicious."

David became more aware of his body's needs—the need for more hydration, for more movement in order to feel good.

The other question he explored was, "How do you expect to live when all of the food you eat is dead?" So, he went on a campaign of only eating live food. He also eliminated all the things that were toxic in his life. He eliminated TV, news, coffee, his beloved cigars, his beloved wine. He actually followed this practice for 5 years. And now, other than coffee, he can eat most of everything. However, it's only a rare occasion that he deviates from his health plan.

David claims that when you are present with yourself, you can more easily make promises and commitments and keep them. He not only demonstrates, but strongly believes, that it's never too late to improve your health. The resilience of the body, mind, and spirit is phenomenal if we just give it a chance. If we just begin to relax. The body truly wants to be healthy. If you give it a little more love and a little more support, you will begin to experience the rewards of your efforts.

For David, getting in touch with his body and health was an outcome from opening up to his spiritual practice. He knew he probably should get healthier. But it wasn't until he learned how to quiet his mind and body that he finally was able to establish a more intimate relationship with his body. Over time, he was able to truly discover what his body needed to be lean, fit, and healthy.

I also interviewed my friends, who I've known for several years: Judi and Jeff Snyder. Both of them had been struggling for many years with their weight, and they were not sure what else they could do.

One of the first things they mentioned was they kept searching and researching for answers.

Judi went to an integrative physician who had her try an elimination diet. Judi discovered that there were foods that did not work with her body. She then researched further and discovered she was insulin resistant. Judi also found out that the older we get, the more challenged we can be to process carbs. She was now mainly low carb, although still having some fruit.

Jeff also did his own research and found out he too had become insulin resistant.

It was when they implemented a Keto protocol, combined with intermittent fasting, as well as exercise, that the pounds began melting away. In a relatively short period of time, they both lost a tremendous amount of weight. Judi lost 85 pounds. Jeff lost 90.

What I like about what they both did was: they did their research. They consulted with a physician who specialized in weight issues. They found the foods that worked for them. They found a structure that worked for them. And I also liked that they prioritized their health as they would any business meeting or project. They put their health first. They organized their time to know what they were going to eat and when they were going to exercise.

And they made sure they treated themselves like their best client, which they are. None of us would ever consider not showing up for an appointment with a client or customer. So, why do we do that with ourselves?

One last aspect that I really liked: they became accountability partners for each other. This also made a big difference in their commitment and ability to stick with their way of caring for themselves. This formula loaded them for success.

So, what might you need? What kind of support might help you? What can you begin doing differently?

And there is one more component that needs to be considered: your emotional health.

I have one more person who I was inspired to interview.

I met Dr. Kevin Ross Emery many years ago. We were both part of the faculty with CEO Space International (CEO Space is a business growth organization mentoring business owners). Like many, Kevin had struggled with his weight for many, many years.

But a few years ago, Kevin discovered he had a health issue with his heart. It was a wake-up call. But it still took some time before he actually did something more about it. Kevin had recently gotten married, and his husband has diabetes, so health was important to both of them.

What I like about Kevin's approach is he first did his research. Even more significant, Kevin focused on the emotional issues that were contributing to his overeating and not taking better care of his body. (I believe this is the main reason people gain back their weight. They have not yet dealt with their core issues contributing to being overweight).

Kevin recognized the importance of doing the "inner work"—healing the emotional issues contributing to being unhealthy.

Kevin found himself more committed. He was rapidly approaching 60 and knew taking care of his body was even more important as we age. Kevin wanted to make sure that not only his 60s were good, but all the remaining years of his life.

And for any of us to achieve optimal health, you have to find out "why" this is important to you. For David, he literally took a spiritual vow. For Kevin, he knew heart disease, high cholesterol, and diabetes ran in his family, and he did not want that for himself.

Whatever your "why" may be, dig deep until you find it. And then, write it in a place where you can see it every day. Because we know there will be days that you will not want to get out of bed and exercise. There will be days that are more stressful, and you may be tempted to eat foods that don't support your body and your efforts.

But the more you have a plan of action, especially what you can do in times of stress, the better off you will be.

Please remember: This is a journey. Whatever your circumstances, just start. Just one step in the right direction will help you build back your confidence. With time, you will create a beautiful momentum and eventually achieve your desired results.

The more steps you take, the easier it will be.

But it's important to take a step.

What is *your* next step going to be?

EXERCISE: This exercise was given to me many years ago from the Avatar community, called "Care for the Animal." This exercise allows you to demonstrate love for your body. The power of love is transformational. I encourage you to do this exercise daily.

Find a time where you can be in quiet and begin relaxing. Your body is like a newborn child, totally dependent on you for care. Without your efforts, it cannot survive. If you have ever held a newborn child, your heart overflows with love.

You are going to treat your body with a tender, loving touch. Look at your forearm with love. Gently stroke it, showering it with feelings of love. Move your hand to your upper arm, caressing it, gently stroking it, sending that part of your body lots of love. Continue this process with each part of your body. When you finish, just sit there for a few moments, feeling all the love you have poured into your body.

A daily practice is what works best. With time you will begin noticing a healthier relationship with your body. I have seen people lose weight and/or restore their health by just doing this one exercise.

(The Miraculous Living Method will aid you in your journey of restoring your health. You can also inquire about my next Loving Yourself Lean program.)

Dear God:

I am blessed to have been given this gift of life. I am blessed to have been given such an extraordinary body. I know I have used my body as a scapegoat for other issues in my life. I now learn to love and appreciate my body more and more with each day. Help me fill myself with love. Assist me to care for my body as my new best friend. Help me restore my body to be healthy, full of energy and vitality. I am forever grateful for this body I've been given.

Chapter 11

It's Never Too Late to Attract and Be In Love

In my life and work, it's very important for me to be living a life with integrity. That means being in alignment with who I am and being truthful in the way I live my life.

For many years, one of my areas of specialization has been working with singles to attract love. Yet, I became single again, so I was self-conscious that I was not in a relationship.

So, I began leaning into the area of my life that I had not yet fulfilled, preparing myself to welcome love.

I believe that if you have a desire in your heart...it is

your truth. I believe your desires are planted within you to help you learn, grow, and evolve. It's like a carrot dangling in front of you, tempting you, having you move forward to fulfill that desire.

However, when life brings disappointments, heartache, and pain, it is sometimes too easy to squash and disconnect from that desire. And this can definitely be true when it comes to love.

So, wanting that special relationship is your truth. No ands, ifs, or buts, about it.

Next, we're going to focus on waking up your desire. You may not even realize you may be pushing that desire away, because it can be painful recognizing what is missing in your life.

I know I would occasionally catch myself feeling a bit cynical. My friends had encouraged me to create a profile and engage in online dating. As I was doing this, I remember having a conversation with God. I remember saying, "God, you and I know it is highly unlikely that I will meet the man you have chosen for me online; however, I am doing this to demonstrate that I am open to however we might meet."

So, I began the online experience.

I'll never know the exact reason, but I definitely was not attracting the quality of man that I would be interested in. Also, I was attracting men much older than me, which I was not interested in—especially at this time of my life.

I knew if I was not attracting the quality of man that would be a good "fit" for me, there was probably something inside of me that was preventing that from happening.

You see, we are masterful at manifesting exactly what we believe. And if you want to know what is going on inside of you (your thoughts and emotions), just look at what you've created in your life.

If you have an awesome life, your inner conversations and how you view the world is obviously in alignment with what you want to create and experience.

However, if there are areas that you are missing or that are not working, then the place to begin is with you.

So, at that point in my life, I took myself off the dating site and decided to work on me. I knew that there must be a place within me that was not allowing love to come into my life.

When I first met Anne, she had heard me on a radio program focusing on relationships. Anne was 52 at the time and had never been married, although she had always wanted a husband. As we began working together, it was clear how Anne had protected herself from hurt and disappointment. She also had a very successful career as an engineer, now managing a very large team of engineers.

In Anne's words: "As we worked together, Wendy helped me to believe that this desire would be fulfilled. She encouraged me to be very clear about what I wanted from a relationship, also realizing this meant some men would 'disappear' when they didn't meet my criteria. This helped me stay positive through the online dating process. I also needed to understand feminine energy and learn to 'receive.' Being an elder child, working in a male-dominated industry for 30 years, and living on my own since my mid-20s had left me very independent and somewhat masculine in my approach to life."

Not too long after Anne and I began working together, she happened to mention that it might be time to explore a new job. She had been with the same company for over 20 years, and she felt she was at the end of her opportunities. I remember uttering an "uh oh," meaning that sometimes other things need to change before actually attracting love into your life.

And this was the case with Anne. She had been living in Canada and was thinking it was time to move back to Australia. I encouraged her to dust off her resume and explore recruiters in the areas of Australia she was willing to live.

Just a couple of weeks later, out of the "blue," Anne was contacted by a recruiter—and not one of the ones she had already explored. There was a position they were asking her to consider. And, believe it or not, it was in the same town in which she had grown up.

It probably will not surprise you that Anne got the job. And, it was, unfortunately, a turbulent transition. I was now praying that this guy better show up soon, since her boss and work environment were very toxic, and she was really being challenged in this new position.

Anne recalls: "One Saturday I was out walking and challenged God about why this was taking so long. Speaking to God, 'I believe love is out there for me, so how can I trust You when You haven't answered this prayer for so many years? I'm willing to do whatever it takes, even learn to play golf!' (I was walking past a golf course at the time). During the next few days, I started engaging online with a guy who got through my screening questions, so I suggested we meet for coffee. He was a little hesitant, as it was his first experience with online dating after 34 years of marriage. Over coffee, we discovered that I was attending the church he grew up in and we knew a lot of people in common, which reassured both of us in different ways. We discovered that the same weekend I'd been challenging God, he had been asking God how to meet women and just happened to pick the same dating site that I was on. We continued to date and enjoy time together, and on the anniversary of our first coffee, he proposed! It turned out that I didn't have to learn golf, but I am learning to love fishing and camping, and he is learning to love ballroom dancing."

Jeff and Anne were married on June 13, 2020. And a small gift of COVID is that they streamed their wedding, and I was able to attend. Very special, for sure.

Another client of mine was Lisa Lent. Lisa had been referred to me because she was having some challenges with her business. I remember Lisa so clearly, since she was my first client after moving to San Diego in 2013. However, during our very first conversation, I also discovered Lisa really wanted a relationship. The way I work with people is to explore all areas of life (I have 10 categories we explore).

In Lisa's case, she was struggling with her business *and* she was truly wanting a relationship (although she had not brought that up until I asked). For many years, Lisa had been a flight attendant. She literally had the luxury of traveling the globe. But she also saw the toll flying was having on her as well as the other crew. She eventually invented a nutritional product and started her own business.

So, we began working together.

Lisa was like a sponge, taking in all she could to transform herself and her life. And within four months of us working together, she met Paul, whom she would later refer to as her life partner.

Lisa and I continued to stay in touch over the years and I was delighted at how happy she and Paul were.

And then came a conversation that no one wants to receive. Lisa had contracted cancer. She fought long and hard, and unfortunately passed away August 31, 2020.

Lisa and Paul had almost 7 years together. Their time together was rich and filled with many adventures.

Paul was with her during those very challenging times, as well as her mother and sister Stephanie.

Lisa is a testament to realizing there are no guarantees in life. You hopefully will live a long, healthy, and prosperous life. But we never know. I would never have guessed in a million years that Lisa would pass away at the young age of 49.

So, please, don't waste any more time. If there is something you want, go for it!

It will be a wonderful way to honor Lisa. It will be even more significant as a gesture to honor yourself.

What I love about the Miraculous Living Method is that you do not have to actually know what's keeping love away.

There is so much more we know today about how to transform your life.

So, let's make sure you are positioned to attract love into your life...now!

As for me, I continued to work on myself. Two of my girlfriends had an intervention with me, encouraging me to start dating again. Once again, I enrolled in an online dating service.

Once again, I was still attracting men much older than me. I always thanked them for reaching out to me; however, at this time in my life, I was interested in having a relationship with someone closer to my own age. Then, I wished them success in finding their relationship.

I had even marked the end of my online dating membership on my calendar. I wanted to show God I was open, but I happen to be a person who does not like to throw my money away.

However, on June 21, 2019, my life was about to change.

I received a notification that someone from the website had emailed me. I went to his profile. If he was telling the truth, he was just a year older than me. *Nice.* If his photos were recent, he looked good. I read his profile. He sounded interesting. He seemed to write clearly, so that was a good start.

He looked and sounded good. However, I must admit my suspicious nature showed up, praying that he was not a scammer.

So, I returned that email and we set up a time to chat the next day.

I don't remember the conversation, but it was enough that I was willing to set up a time to meet. We made arrangements to meet the next day for coffee.

Our first meeting was pleasant, certainly no fireworks. In fact, I was wondering if he might be nervous. Like I said, it was pleasant, but no great shakes. But after our time together was over, there was something within me that felt I needed to give this man another chance.

So I did.

And we met the second time for dinner.

Again, it was a pleasant start, a very neutral kind of experience. However, about halfway through our time together, I found myself becoming interested—even a bit intrigued.

When we finished our meal, the man—John—walked me to my car, giving me a very polite hug.

So now he asked for a third date, this time requesting to come pick me up and go for a movie and dinner. (I had enough confirmed information about him that I felt safe for him to come to my home). I still didn't know how he felt or if he had me in the "friend" zone (since I do enjoy meeting people and developing friendships). I wanted greater clarity by the end of this third date. I was hoping he would at least hold my hand.

Well, the man who showed up at my house was completely different than the man I had been with previously! This man was animated, more outgoing. He took my hand as we walked to the movie theater and held my hand throughout the entire movie (guess I wasn't just in the friend zone). And before dinner, outside Vons grocery store, we had our first kiss (I know, not the most romantic—but memorable for us).

It's now 21 months since that first email and I am beyond grateful for having this man in my life. We share many of the same values. We enjoy doing many of the same things. And, even though these past months we have had to deal with COVID and "shelter in place," I am forever grateful that I get to shelter with him.

I'm sharing all of this, since first, I am eating my words that I would not find love online! Second, I'm very grateful that I gave myself more time to get to know John after a couple of times getting together. If I would have based my decision on our first meeting, I would have passed up a wonderful man and relationship.

So, at the wonderful ages of 69 and 70, we are blessed

to have each other and this quality relationship in our lives.

And there is one more story that I would like to share:

"I was married to my wife for thirteen years and our marriage was getting stale. I mentioned to her that we seemed to be more like brother and sister. Since she was not happy either, we decided to divorce. It was very amicable, and we kept in touch regularly, even though we both ended up finding someone else. This lasted almost three and a half years when my relationship fell apart. Around the same time, my ex-wife's relationship also faltered. I was not thinking about reuniting with my ex, but she was all for giving it another try. After living together for a couple of years, we remarried and were together for another thirteen years. At this point, we were living through our retirements, living in our dream home, and we were set 'forever,' or so I thought.

"Then one day my wife came home and told me she wanted a divorce. At the age of 67, it was devastating. Shattering the life we built for over three decades hurt badly, and going through all the upheaval was exhausting and I felt lost. To be married twice to the same woman and believing we would be together forever, to then be confronted with yet another divorce, was something I had never contemplated.

"I thought it was over for me. And I certainly never thought I would find myself contemplating dating again. After all, I hadn't dated in over 30 years (the relationship I had after my first divorce was an arrangement made by an acquaintance).

"So, I did not date for almost two years. But after being encouraged by my two life-long friends' wives, I joined a dating site. I was a "fish out of water," to say the least. It took me three months to finally go on my first date, and that was a mess. I called my date after lunch and told her I was just not ready to date. After some time, I continued to look for that woman who could give me the trusting, loyal, comforting, and loving companionship I was truly missing. After three other dates that went nowhere, I was discouraged and almost gave up on trying to find someone.

"Then, one day, I reached out to a woman because I liked her profile. I sent a message to her, saying that it seemed we were both looking for the same things. Our first meeting was a coffee date. It was 'okay,' not that great, but we decided to meet again. I was somewhat preoccupied that day because I was traveling the next day (and I also had rushed to meet her from a previous lunch date). When I returned from my trip, we arranged our next date. This was a dinner date and it lasted three hours. We talked a lot about our past and told our stories. I never thought it would amount to much, but I still decided to have another date. I was curious, but not sure if this would be the right match for me. But our next date is when we both found a more special connection, and we have now had many more dates of all different kinds.

"And I can now say, for real, 'it's never too late.' We have been together for almost two years, and I am happier than I could ever believe. And to think I am in the best and most fulfilling relationship with a writer who believes 'it's never too late,' since *my* Darling wrote this book." - John Anella

Now...it's your turn!

What I love about John's journey is how important it is to be sensitive to how vulnerable most of us feel when meeting others and hoping to make a true, beautiful connection. I will be forever grateful John did not give up. He is such a kind, generous, loyal, and really good man. And he happens to be a lot of fun to be around.

And I know with every fiber of my being, there *is* someone for you too.

It is truly never too late for love...*ever*!

Do what you can to release the wounds of your heart and mind. Fill yourself with God's love each and every day. *Trust* that there are perfect partners for you *now* (yes, there are more than one). They are most likely trying to find you, and they want you as much as you want them.

And open yourself to *receive*! When I work with people, being able to receive is one of the first areas I assist them with to open up. With the exception of only one person I have ever worked with (and I happen to be in a relationship with him), every single person has been constricted in some way to receive. Obviously, that impacts all areas of your life, but for now, we are talking about love.

Open up and let the heavens shower you with their love, allowing yourself to be deeply nourished. Then, open yourself up to draw love to you.

Dear God:

There is nothing I desire more than to attract and create a beautiful, rich, and fulfilling relationship. My heart and soul hunger for this connection. My life yearns to be shared. Please come inside me, heal any wounds that are present, keeping my Beloved away. Help restore my faith that it's simply a matter of time before my Beloved and I first meet. Allow me to feel this person in my heart and to know, it's simply a matter of time. I am grateful for this gift you send, the gift of my True Love.

Chapter 12

It's Never Too Late to Replenish and Restore Your Relationship

Over the years, I have been blessed to work with couples to support them in restoring their relationship.

So, what happens that so many couples drift apart, while others thrive?

It was very easy for me to decide who I wanted to interview for this chapter. I am blessed with some very special friends. Adam and Randi Markel happen to be two of them. Adam and I originally met at CEO Space International, a business growth organization, where we were both part of their faculty. We had an immediate connection, and he and his wife became fast friends with me (we conveniently live 10 minutes from each other).

Before John came into my life, I found it fascinating that my inner circle of friends included a small group of men. I have always had really good female friends, but having a few close men friends was new for me. I referred to them as my San Diego Posse. I also found it interesting, and as an added bonus, they were all in very healthy and happy marriages.

I happened to be the single one in our group. And I very much valued how the couples would include me. It was nice to be around couples who were in happy and healthy relationships. It also gave me hope that there would be a day when I would be part of a couple too.

Adam and Randi met in college in 1985. They met in a Child Psychology class together. Randi was an education major, so this class was important to her. Turns out Adam was taking this class because it was a "filler." In fact, he came directly from his trampoline class (tough life!). On their first date, they talked into the wee hours. Looking back, Randi knew that very first night she had met someone special.

Adam and Randi married in July of 1990, on the eve of Randi's college graduation. At the time of our interview, they had recently celebrated their 31st year of marriage (being together for 36 years).

In addition to having a happy, healthy marriage, they have birthed and raised 4 very special children, now ranging in ages from 20 to 28. This past year they experienced life as empty nesters, although two of their children still live locally, the other two still in California.

When asked what they focused on to keep their love alive, healthy, resilient, and exciting, these were Randi's comments:

1. **Romance**. Randi spoke of how Adam is very romantic and works really hard to be so. He doesn't take for granted that she will know how he feels. He always works at showing her, whether she reciprocates or not.

2. **Build Each Other Up.** Randi spoke of how important it is to support each other. First, find ways to build each other up. Then, find things that nourish yourself. Randi shared that early in their relationship she resented when Adam would go off by himself and do things she did not enjoy. Eventually she learned that the times Adam reads, swims, surfs, and does things that make him feel

great, he shows up as the man she adores. (She also discovered that when he did not do these things, he was more of a crab and even resented that she didn't want him doing those things). A really important point: as much as Randi wants Adam to love her, she wants him to love himself. She learned the best thing she can do is build him up and support him in doing everything that makes him feel great.

3. **Nourish Yourself.** Randi was able to realize the importance of finding ways to nourish yourself by the examples Adam demonstrated to her. She got to explore and find ways that made her feel great and nourished, allowing her to show up as her greater self and be in their relationship at an even playing field. She discovered embodiment work and went on retreats. Eventually, Randi began leading retreats, and Adam supported her 100%. This was a true moment for Randi, since she finally understood that with both of them feeling so full and nourished, they were able to be there fully for each other.

4. **Gratitude.** Adam and Randi have always had a practice of gratitude. She also acknowledged that as an older couple, it has become even more important. And it wasn't as if their lives were a "cakewalk." They faced many challenges: health challenges, career and business challenges. And even though they had

a solid relationship, Randi shared that there were times she even questioned, "Are we going to be able to survive this?" But gratitude kept them grounded in their hearts.

5. **Basecamp.** This is where Randi and Adam intentionally create space for their relationship. Just like when you are climbing a mountain, basecamp is where you set up camp, where you rest, a place of refuge so you can continue your climb. After 9/11, they were devastated. Adam and Randi were living on the east coast and knew many people who perished in the Twin Towers. The world was literally tumbling all around them. They used basecamp to help get grounded, breathe, and reset. They would ask each other, "What do you need?" And they would create a plan together.

"Whether it's big moments in our lives or moments when we want to slow down and catch our breath, basecamp serves us well. When we are in California, our basecamp is our yoga practice. We also set beautiful intentions, how we set up our day, and talk about it."

As empty-nesters, they have been resetting what their life is going to look like now.

Randi shares: "As we practice gratitude and basecamp, I have become more comfortable in my own skin. It relieves my head of any worry or stress. Figuring things out together allows me to fill my cup up too, no matter what the circumstances. I also believe that if you don't have gratitude in your life, you will be challenged to be truly fulfilled. And without gratitude alive in your relationship, your relationship will also be challenged to be fulfilled. We also value the practice of setting intentions in our relationship and all areas of our lives."

As you can see, Randi and Adam have created certain practices and rituals. Years ago, for their anniversary, they wrote a letter to each other as if it was their 75th wedding anniversary. Adam wrote a beautiful love letter. And then Randi created a mini vision board, where they were going to be celebrating, who was going to be there. They still are talking about that now. They found it to be a powerful exercise, as well as a beautiful model for their kids, to see that you have to make an effort.

Randi and Adam have another ritual for their anniversary. Wherever they are, they always go someplace to buy a card. They write beautiful, loving messages and exchange them while having dessert.

Another practice is they meditate at night together, in bed, before going to sleep. Sometimes they'll have music on, sometimes using guided meditations.

And, lastly, they make sure to set time aside to be together, whether it's taking a walk, going to yoga, or doing absolutely nothing.

Randi and Adam were fortunate to discover these things and practice them regularly. You may now have some additional ideas of what you want to do differently.

I also suggest you explore *The 5 Love Languages by Gary Chapman.* I use this with the couples I work with, and it is truly amazing how using this can begin to create greater connection, understanding, and intimacy.

Another couple I interviewed are my good friends, Veronica and Steve Farber. They met in 1999 on what was then called AOL Love. These were back in the days of early dating apps. Steve is a professional speaker and was traveling a lot, so a friend had recommended he explore online dating. He confesses his early experiences were not great. His biggest objection was that pictures were not matching the women he was meeting. So, he ended up actually saying something in his profile about "even though looks are not everything, please make sure your pictures are current." Veronica sent him a picture, and he really liked how she looked.

After speaking on the phone, they decided to get together and ended up having a 3-hour lunch.

Steve confessed that if you would have looked at any analytical approach to their relationship, you would never think it would work. They have very different backgrounds. But their core values were very congruent: Family, Fidelity, Commitment. Plus, Steve states that they had a very strong connection and they just "knew" they were to be together. Yet, after getting married (they had 6 kids between them), they also found that they had different approaches to parenting. Plus, Veronica was not used to being with an entrepreneur (aka, fluctuating income), which created additional stress. Steve had also convinced Veronica to quit her job and assist him with his business, which was the day before 9/11. More stress.

So, the first few years of their marriage were more challenging, but both feel that their core values and a deep special connection are what brought them through all of that.

And, with time, Steve and Veronica have also become more aligned on what was previously their different issues.

Steve and Veronica both expressed how they are advocates and huge fans for each other. They find they have a good balance between the two of them. Steve is an idea person. If he has a great idea, Veronica will be the one to ask many questions about how this could work, or not.

Steve states, "If Veronica was not a believer in me, there would be no way we could be business partners, let alone married. For us, being business partners has worked very well. There is no sense of separation. It's all one life and there is a lot of power with that. Being 'all in' together really works for us."

One of the greatest gifts of their relationship is that they laugh a lot. Veronica shares how easy Steve makes her laugh, and vice versa.

And even in these uncertain times (this is during the pandemic), they are now brainstorming different options of "what if."

One nice thing that came from the pandemic is they began taking walks together, which they had never done before.

They also really love their kids. They love the times when they are all together and continue to stay interested and involved with what's going on in their lives.

For Steve and Veronica, arguments and/or

disagreements are typically minor and short-lived. They typically don't get very emotional. In the early days, Veronica admits they were quite emotional: issues around kids, other ways they were continuing to work out differences as they continued to get to know each other. Neither of them likes for there to be dissension between them. So, they have found ways to forgive and move on. They found what is most important and works is to figure out what they need, what to do about it, and move on.

When I asked Steve what he might suggest to other couples, he was a bit hesitant, recognizing that this is so specific to each individual's scenario. That said, he suggested to be willing to be uncomfortable in a conversation, especially when you don't want to be in the conversation.

Great suggestion. I have always believed that the "mischief" in a relationship does not typically occur for what is said, but for what is not. It's important to learn to express yourself, especially when it may feel more challenging or make you feel more vulnerable. If you don't express yourself, these thoughts and feelings will build up, and eventually you risk projectile vomiting these pent-up feelings all over your partner. It's how disagreements can occur. It's how you also can more easily lose that sweet connection with your partner.

The bottom line: Steve and Veronica talk about how important love is in a relationship. They also recognize how important it is to like their partner as a person. Liking someone is not as subject to change. You may not feel the magical attraction all of the time; however, if you like someone, that's what will sustain a relationship. Without that, you might doubt the strength and stability of the relationship.

Steve admits that there has never been a time that he felt he didn't like Veronica. Never. The "in love" thing is different. That can be more of a wave.

And their last piece of advice: Find ways to laugh.

So, what can you begin doing to create a stronger connection between you and your partner? Are you needing a conversation? Are you wanting to take a closer look at your life and your relationship to create clear intentions for now and your future? Are you in need of coming up with new and fun things to do together? Whatever it may be, identify one or two things you can begin doing now.

Dear God:

I miss the deep love my sweetheart and I once shared. I no longer remember what happened that we have reached this point in our relationship. Please guide me to find ways for us to connect with each other, to love each other, to support each other. Help us find our way back to love. Help us find new ways to love, to connect, to learn, to grow and trust. I believe we can find our way back to each other. Thank you for all the love and support you provide each and every day.

Chapter 13

It's Never Too Late
to Start a Family

I had to include this chapter in the book.

Good friends of mine, Esther Wildenberg and Cheri Tree, were married and wanted children. Esther had been in a serious accident several years ago, so she was unable to carry a child. At the wonderful age of 45, Cheri volunteered.

They picked out their donor and used Esther's eggs. Cheri got pregnant with twins. Unfortunately, early in the pregnancy, they lost the babies. Understandably, it was a devastating loss for them both.

But they did not give up.

One year later, they tried the process again. And, once again, it worked. This time Cheri was able to carry the pregnancy successfully. There were some minor complications, requiring Cheri to be on 24-hour bedrest. And even though he was born 10 weeks premature, Kai is a very happy and healthy little boy. Cheri and Esther are totally in love and thrilled with their amazing son. And it is also a miracle since Cheri was just weeks shy of turning 47 when she delivered Kai.

And I know other women who have successfully conceived and carried a baby in their 40s.

I wanted to include this chapter, since there are so many people still desiring to have a family, and they are past what society has previously defined as a "natural" age range to start a family.

In Esther and Cheri's case, they were able to use in vitro fertilization.

But that is not an option for many people.

However, there are *so* many babies and young children who would *love* to be adopted, who would *love* to have a real home.

And I want to share one more story, a miraculous

story. In fact, even how this story came to me was miraculous. I had almost finished re-reading my book and was planning on turning it over to my publisher that day. I had known Candice Hozza for several years and we were together in a small business meeting that morning. Candice happened to share part of her story with someone else. I asked Candice if I could interview her that day, and we both had time to allow that to happen.

Candice was married and already had given birth to her daughter. Yet, she longed for another child. However, her husband did not. This created a hole in Candy's heart for 10 years.

Yet, in 1993, long before much of what I am about to share, Candice actually received an image in her "mind's eye" of her baby boy being birthed and being a part of their lives. She fell in love with him that very morning.

But Candice started having health issues, bleeding excessively. It turned out Candice had uterine cancer and needed immediate surgery. The only treatment was to remove her uterus, preventing her from having another child.

Candice consulted other doctors, who all made the same recommendation. If she didn't have the surgery,

Candice risked having the cancer spread through her ovaries and into her body, putting her life at risk.

Candice was torn. Yet, she scheduled her surgery.

But she had another experience, a first for her. She was in a hotel room by herself, where her husband was having a business meeting. This was an opportunity for them to try to begin recovering their relationship.

Candice suddenly heard, as if someone was in the room, "You still have a uterus." She looked around since the voice seemed very real. She had no idea what this meant, and her surgery was now a month away.

So, Candice did the only thing she knew how to do: she turned to prayer. Both she and her mother-in-law decided she needed a miracle.

Candice was now scheduled for her pre-surgery appointment. While there, she told the doctor she just could not go through with the surgery. After talking about all of this, her doctor finally offered her an option: one more biopsy. And if the biopsy was still conclusive, hopefully not worse, would she please agree to the surgery? Candice agreed.

It was a couple of weeks later and both she and her husband were at this appointment. The doctor looked at both of them in complete amazement. There was absolutely no evidence of cancer.

He said he had never seen anything like this before and found himself writing a prescription for prenatal vitamins. He didn't know if they would be able to conceive a child but encouraged the two of them to take advantage of this window of opportunity, because they had just received a miracle.

Candice explained that she did not really think about that baby boy very often. She just knew that she had been shown this boy and lived with complete faith and trust.

Candice became pregnant approximately two years after that appointment. She gave birth to their miracle baby boy. In fact, Candice wanted to name their son William John. However, one evening, her very conservative husband announced that he had heard that their son's name was to be Phoenix, a biblical name that means "coming out of the ashes to give others hope."

There are even more miraculous details to this story. The TLC Channel actually featured their miracle story. You can go to www.candicehozza.com/media to watch.

I recognize Candice's story is very extreme and miraculous. I would never recommend putting your life at risk. However, Candice and her son Phoenix are another example of the miracles that are possible in our lives each and every day.

Of course, none of us knows what the future holds. You could even inherit children through your new relationship.

So, if having a family is something that is truly a desire in your heart, you have to know that a child is calling out for you to be their mom or dad.

Dear God:

For a long time, I have prayed for a family I could call my own. Please help me find that beautiful soul who is also seeking me. Thank you for choosing this child for me. Thank you for choosing me for this child. I pray we find each other soon. I know this will be a blessing for us all.

Chapter 14

It's Never Too Late to Make Your Mark

It is hard for me to believe how many years have passed in my life. I have much to be grateful for. Yet, there is still so much I want to accomplish before my time is up here on Earth. At 69 years, I have no intention of retiring. I love what I do.

That said, I can feel the desire to have even greater impact than I have had up until now.

So, I definitely believe that if you still desire to have some greater level of contribution and/or impact, it clearly is *never* too late.

Grandma Moses didn't start painting until the age of 78. One of her paintings sold for over a million dollars.

Peter Roget created the first thesaurus when he was 73 years old. He was trained as a medical doctor and had an obsession with words—especially words that had the same meaning. The most popular thesaurus still bears his name.

Judy Dench was in her 60s when her film career took off.

Harland Sanders found himself broke at 65. Then, things began working out when he sold his first Kentucky Fried Chicken franchise in 1952.

Ray Kroc had passed his 50th birthday when he bought his first McDonald's in 1961.

Duncan Hines wrote his first hotel and food guides at age 55. At 73, he licensed the right to use his name to the company that developed Duncan Hines cake mixes.

And there are thousands of other stories, possibly millions, of people who didn't find their stride to make their mark much later in life.

Have you ever considered how you want to leave your footprint, after you are gone? The legacy you want to leave behind?

I know when I began to explore that, it brought even greater meaning to the work I do, to the gifts I have received. It would be wonderful to know that my programs and processes could live on beyond my life.

Now, I want you to explore this for yourself.

EXERCISE: *I want you to imagine that you have just passed away and are sitting in the lap of God. You are asked to do a "life review." What this means is you are to write out the highlights of your life. These are to include both the challenges that you overcame as well as your accomplishments. If there were regrets, what might those have been? And what did you learn from them? What do you see as the legacy of your life that will live on after you are gone?*

Get out your journal and write away! See what flows out of your heart and pen. You may be surprised.

How did this exercise make you feel? Did you gain more clarity on the direction of your life, how you would like to leave your mark?

It's never too late to leave your mark on the world. But time is ticking away, so it's time to make it happen.

What if all your life experiences have brought you to this very moment in time to finally pursue an idea, a dream, a "something" that has been churning inside you for a very long time?

YOUR TIME IS NOW!

My former client, Diane Forster, was at a crossroads in her life. It was the late fall of 2014. She had been a successful Account Executive with Disney/ABC Television Group in Chicago. When we met, Diane had been divorced for a year and her twins were in their senior year of high school.

Diane knew she was ready for a change. She knew she wanted to speak, coach, and write books and programs. She also wanted to move from Chicago to San Diego.

During our first day working together (my clients get a bonus of a one-day retreat day with me), we were able to outline what her vision was, her mission, and the steps that would be necessary to make that all happen. Her first concern was how she would navigate the change financially, which we also were able to figure out. Diane made the decision to soak up this last year with her children before they went off to college.

Then, after her children left, she put her house up for sale. Her first contract fell through. Her second contract fell through literally at the last minute, as the movers were arriving and she was moving to San Diego. This was September of 2015. She still moved. Diane took the first six weeks in San Diego to regroup and replenish herself. She had faith that her home would sell, which it did in December, her third contract. Diane also felt this period was an opportunity to strengthen and demonstrate her faith and commitment.

In a very short time, Diane immersed herself in trainings (in her first year, she shared, she spent 33 weekends in a variety of trainings). She began coaching clients. She wrote and published her first book. She started speaking and having a lot of interviews on radio and podcasts. She was working with more clients. She also launched her own podcast. Then, she launched, *I Have Today with Diane Forster* TV show, which is now streaming live. She has hosted retreats in her home as well as live virtual events. Diane also won the Global Excellence Award, Life Coach of the Year in California from *Luxe Life Magazine*.

Diane's commitment and mission is to see that one billion women who don't know their self-worth discover their true divinity, power, and purpose.

When asked about her recommendations to those who are still wanting to make their special mark, Diane said: "You are going to grow at the pace that suits you, that's best for you. Anything faster than that, you are not ready for it. I happen to be a driven person. If it's not working, tweak it, fix it, or move on. And having that attitude only comes with time and experience. Whatever you want, you can absolutely have it. It takes clarity, focus, and direction. Be very clear on what you want, stay focused on it, and keep moving forward. You *will* get there."

Diane has made tremendous progress in just a few short years. And, as she mentioned, she is a very driven person. But I also agree, it's very important to go at your own pace, doing what works best for you. And be willing to take your next step.

What step will you take? If there is something you have noodled for a long time, take a step. If you need to do some research, that's a step. No matter how small that step is, it is a step. More times than not, that first step or two is the hardest. If you just take a tiny step and continue to take some tiny steps, you will find yourself making significant progress before you know it. And progress helps to build your confidence and assists you in gaining momentum.

It's like writing a book. Thinking about writing a book can feel rather daunting. When I was getting ready to write my first book, I could not even imagine what I could possibly say that would fill all those pages that eventually became a book. It's what kept me from making progress in the beginning.

However, when I chunked down my writing to chapters and was simply willing to start a chapter, I started seeing the progress I was making little by little. In fact, I was able to write my first book in a little less than 5 weeks, only working on it part-time.

So, *please,* get really honest with yourself.

If you could wave your magic wand, what is the one *thing that you would really love to experience still in your life? How would you like to make your mark? What might you like your legacy to be?*

My philosophy: Do what works, and do it now!

So, what are you going to do now?

Dear God:

I want to thank you for this magnificent life you have given me. I have so much to be grateful for. I know there have been many struggles, but I also know I still have many opportunities remaining. Help me to realize what is best for me to achieve during this next phase of my life. Help guide me to take positive and productive steps. Help me realize, value, and appreciate that my life matters and that I still have time to achieve my deepest desires. Thank you for believing in me, guiding me, and supporting me.

Chapter 15

It's Never Too Late to Create Wealth

This is typically a big issue for many people: money!

Much of my life is defined before my accident and after my accident. Before my accident, life was easy. If I wanted a job, I got it. I had opportunities just show up. However, after my accident, everything seemed foreign. Everything felt like a hurdle. I was hurting and felt very lost.

And I knew how I generated income was going to be an important part in both my learning and my teaching. And that has certainly been true.

For many years, I found myself fascinated with people

who seem to be able to manifest what they want with ease and speed. I no longer believed that you just had to work long, hard hours to become successful. I believe that when you get clear on your gifts, your skills and talents, and how you are going to contribute to others, you can tap into the "flow" of life, which allows you to connect to those you can serve and support—as well as those that can serve and support you. Of course, when you are doing something that has greater meaning for you, more than just a paycheck, those extra hours don't feel like "work." And, yes, it still requires action.

Devorah Leah Siegel's story represents many, many women. Leah had been married for over 14 years and had 4 children. She felt the rug had been pulled out from her. Her husband wanted a divorce. She scrambled to try to find work and support her family. She was able to get a job in a preschool but struggled to make ends meet. She started to accumulate debt. That's when she knew she had to figure this out.

Leah found a mentor and money coach who took her under her wing. She helped Leah strategize getting out of debt, showed her how the financial world worked from the inside, and empowered her to create her own wealth as a result.

Eventually, Leah was able to leave her job and build her own financial firm. Now, Leah coaches and mentors others, just like what was provided for her, giving others that same chance.

If you happen to be going through a major life transition, Leah offers the following advice:

Take ownership and responsibility for where you are, because it is very easy to blame.

Look at your mistakes and habits. Then, be open to learning from someone who is going to get you in a better place.

You want to be in a position to be able to stand on your own feet, no matter what.

Leah admits that she had a lot of work to do on herself, including learning to allow the Universe to guide and support her.

Leah is now married, and they have been together for 7 years. As it turns out, she ended up mentoring her husband and he now practices in her business.

Leah is most proud of the fact that she is now a confident and optimistic person. This has led her to be around other people that support her in being the best version of herself. Leah is grateful that she is now able to be an inspiration to people, inspiring and providing hope.

So, no matter what your circumstances, you can definitely turn your life around and create wealth.

I have another miraculous "turnaround" story to share with you. I already mentioned Cheri Tree in my chapter on *It's Never Too Late to Start A Family*. But Cheri herself is a bit of a walking miracle. She is a demonstration of how anything is possible when you want something bad enough and you want to make a contribution to the world.

Cheri started out in sales. She admits she was not really good at it. Her first year as a financial consultant, she earned $700. She later earned $18,000. She hired coaches and business mentors, read many books, but she just could not make progress. During this time, Cheri kept wondering what needed to be different. This was also at a time where Cheri lost everything, had mounds of debt, and was now living in a storage unit for 18 months between 2010 to 2012!

However, she kept digging, questioning. And, eventually, she realized that sales was not a number game as she had been taught, but had more to do with someone's personality characteristics. And these personality characteristics influenced buying behaviors. She began to see that there were different types of people, and those personality traits also influenced how they decide to "buy." Eventually, Cheri created a brilliant system, now referred to as BANK.

I asked Cheri what got her through those challenging years. She said, "I knew that I was a champion. I maintained a positive attitude. And I did not allow myself to be defined and become a victim of my circumstances."

Codebreaker Technologies is now an international success. Cheri originally launched her BANK system making CDs in her storage unit. Her first year, she generated $500,000 in sales. Today, Cheri speaks on stages all around the world, along with her wife, co-founder, and President, Esther Wildenberg. They work with organizations, direct sales companies, and entrepreneurs. They now train and certify individuals and organizations to teach and utilize their methodology, build their own BANK business, as well as become a certified BANK coach.

Cheri recommends to never give up. "If your dreams are worth pursuing, no matter what challenges you are faced with, keep going. Dust yourself off, keep a positive mindset, and just go for it."

From "zero to millions." Cheri did it. It is definitely possible.

Cheri and Leah both demonstrated it's possible to achieve wealth, and achieve it in a short period of time.

So, what can you do to continue your journey to create wealth?

1. If you haven't already done so, get clear about your desires. What do you really want?

2. Set goals.

3. Work on your mindset, one of the gifts of using the Miraculous Living Method. Examine these beliefs: I am enough; I believe in me; I believe in the miracles of life; I am worthy of wealth; I deserve phenomenal wealth; I easily and consistently attract financial abundance now; I am living a miraculous life. These are just some of the foundational beliefs that need to be 100% true for you.

4. Spend time in meditation or whatever your spiritual practice may be. Get yourself into an "abundance mindset." Allow yourself to *feel* wealthy.

5. Take action every day, even if it's just a small step, in the direction of your goal.

What created the most dramatic shifts for me was when I worked with my mind and emotions, as well as welcoming God/Spirit/The Universe/Intuition to guide me. When I surrendered to this amazing support, not only did I feel the weight of the world lift from my shoulders, but I also had greater clarity what to do each and every day. I found it easier and easier to take the steps needed. I knew if and when I needed to reach out to someone. I knew when I needed to create a marketing campaign and get the support needed. I knew when I needed to go for a walk to clear my mind and regenerate.

When I got to the point in my life and career that I knew that God is my source, the tides truly began turning, and the flow and life began to increase. I began to amazingly attract people that could help get my work out. I had previously invested in marketing, LinkedIn campaigns, and lots of mentors with minimal results. It was not until I fully embraced that God was my source, my support, and my provider that I noticed a significant difference.

I was able to finally connect to my inner wisdom in a way I had not been able to before. And I continued to use the Miraculous Living Method to keep myself in an open and loving place and stay open to receive.

You need to understand that my life was already pretty

great. Yet once I made this shift, it was as if the waters parted and miracles began happening even more.

This was how I knew how life was supposed to be. I was now finally living it.

Now, I can release the obstacles in others easily and quickly. I assist others in materializing their deepest desires. I am forever grateful.

So, what can you do to increase your wealth?

1. KNOW WHAT YOU WANT TO ACCOMPLISH. What is your financial goal? What is your vision of how you will be living your life?

2. KNOW YOUR NUMBERS. You want to know how much money, on average, are you bringing in each month. If you have your own business and money will fluctuate, look at the last 6 months to get an average.

3. WHAT IS YOUR BUDGET? If you don't already have one, create one. List your financial requirements (rent/mortgage, bills, food, gas, etc.) and your secondary expenses (vitamins/supplements, nutritional products, entertainment). Your third category includes the "it would be nice" items: vacations, clothes, new shoes, etc.

Years ago, I remember keeping a savings envelope and a vacation envelope. It made me feel like I was making progress as I put money into my savings envelope. It gave me hope that there would be a day when I would be able to take a vacation. The amounts were small to start, but it was a start. With time, I was able to put the money into my savings account, but I kept a chart of how the money was to be allocated.

4. GO THROUGH ALL YOUR CHECKS AND CREDIT CARD STATEMENTS to see where you are actually spending your money. Are you sticking within your budget? Or are you going over? How might you be able to adjust your spending?

5. WHAT ABOUT SAVINGS? How good are you at saving money? Every time you receive money, make sure you put some aside for savings. I remember when I was in that very lean time of life, I would earn some money and I would put some of it, in cash, in an envelope that I kept in my desk. I didn't even have enough to open a savings account yet. But it was a start. Soon, I had enough to open that savings account. Later, I began investing. The point is to start! Don't be ashamed, worried, or concerned if you are unable to take 10% or 20% out. Just start. Every little bit makes a difference.

6. MAKE A MIRACULOUS MONEY CHART. (This is particularly helpful for entrepreneurs or those of you who want to bring in extra income). Take a sheet of paper and put it somewhere where you can see it every day. Place the month at the top of the page. For example, you want to generate a minimum of $5,000 a month. Take a sheet of paper, write the month on top (i.e., May, 2020), and your amount. Then, let's say you are paid $300 for services. You would put that amount under the $5,000 and subtract it. Cross out the $5,000 and the $300, then write $4,700. You are showing your brain that you now need at least another $4,700 to fulfill your goal for the month. It works! After some time, if you prefer, you can extend your time to quarterly, 6 months, or annually.

You can also take a similar approach for the number of clients you intend to work with for the year. For example, if you have a goal of 100 new clients, you could make a chart with numbers 1-100. With each new client, cross out the number, starting with 100. Again, you are showing your brain how many more clients you need to reach your goal.

7. LIVE WITH A GENEROUS, SHARING HEART. The concept of sharing your wealth and good fortune has been around for many, many years. Some refer

to this as tithing. I refer to this as "sharing your wealth." There is something special, even magical about finding places to contribute to. It creates the circle of life, in terms of your riches. You receive, and you share your wealth with others. In doing so, it opens up the flow of riches. What is important is to make sure that you do this out of the goodness of your heart, not as a bartering mechanism with God to produce more wealth. At first, this may feel a little awkward, but eventually it feels wonderful. I share my wealth with different organizations. Is there a place in the world that you would like to support? That your contribution, no matter what size, will add value to someone else's life? When you share your wealth, it fills your heart. It feels really good to know that you are impacting the lives of other people who may be going through challenging times. You'll realize what matters to you most.

8. TAKE GUIDED/INSPIRED ACTION! This...is... critical. You may not know how you are going to generate your money. Maybe you do. You want to stay open and "listen" for guidance on what action to take. The more you are able to ask your Inner Guidance System—God, Your Wisdom, whatever you wish to call it—for what it wants you to know and what it wants you to do, make sure you do it. The more you do what you are guided to do, the

more you will be given and the more guidance you will receive. This relationship is so important and valuable to creating your wealth.

Inspired action is different than just any action. You can feel that it's an important step to take. It comes from guidance. It comes from your heart. And even though I'm calling this "inspired" action, you may not always feel completely inspired to take it. Nonetheless, follow your inspiration.

I can remember a time when I was guided to move to south Florida. I had heard of this happening to people, but never would have guessed that this was going to be part of my journey.

I had been living in Dallas. I was consulting and working with private clients. My business had slowed, which can happen. Typically, I take some steps to get things moving again. However, this time I felt I was being guided *not* to do that, to stay still.

I also recall sharing this with my mom and stepfather. I'm sure I had some concern in my voice, since my stepfather very calmly said: "Honey, don't worry. One of these mornings you'll wake up and know exactly what to do."

He was right. That conversation was on a Tuesday in the

mid-90s. That Friday, I woke up with a clear "knowing" that I was to move to south Florida. It was a clear and calm feeling knowing that.

At that time, I was sharing my home with a good friend, and when she came out of her room that morning, I shared with her that I was being guided to move to south Florida. Her immediate response was, "That's great!"

It gets even better.

The home that I was living in had been on the market for sale for almost 1.5 years. I received a call on Saturday that the house was selling with a 2-week closing date.

It was almost as if the heavens were saying: "She's listening. Let's get her out before she changes her mind." I packed up, put all my furniture into storage, and my son and I set off on our adventure to Florida.

I had called my cousins, who lived in Ft. Lauderdale, asking if we could stay with them for a couple of weeks until I was able to find a place to live. That two weeks ended up being a year. We had so much fun, and it was really healthy for me having family around as I began living in south Florida.

Since I did not have much money, I made a promise

to God that I would pay attention and accept offers for work. Within a very short period of time, I was offered an opportunity to sell long-distance to companies. Of course, I said yes. And, I must admit, I was not very good at it. However, it was a start. It also helped me learn my way around my new community since I was calling on companies.

I also attended a meeting where I met someone who became my new best friend. She had a wellness center and hired me to be a receptionist and get her office organized. She also offered me an office where I could begin seeing clients.

I went to the Jewish Community Center in Ft. Lauderdale and shared the various programs I could offer. They wanted me to offer my dating program, which at that time was called Blue Chip Dating (now called "The Miracle of Attracting Love Now"). They did all the advertising; I simply had to show up (my favorite way of doing things). There were over 300 people in attendance and my business went from zero to mach speed.

Then, the Boca Raton Jewish Community Center heard about what I had done in Ft. Lauderdale, and they also wanted me to offer my program to their community.

Meanwhile, I was introduced to someone who was

starting a BNI Networking group. He made the error of sending me to check out another BNI group to see how it worked. Turns out this was a very mature group, and there was no one in my category. So, I joined that group.

Once again, I was getting more clients!

One of the members in the BNI group wrote an article about me in the *South Florida Business Journal*. This was a huge gift, and I was tremendously grateful for it. To my surprise, it was titled: "Our Fairy Godmother Just Landed in South Florida!" The title "Fairy Godmother" has been following me for years. I have had so many other situations where people would refer to me as their personal Fairy Godmother. I don't really think of myself as a Fairy Godmother, but I am both humbled and appreciative that many do. Eventually, I surrendered and appreciated the magic that people were experiencing working with me.

So, by following my heart and my guidance, I was able to turn my life around and generate a lot of new business. One of the reasons that I am certain I was guided to move to south Florida was to heal my relationship with my mom.

My mom and stepfather lived in south Florida for half of the year.

They say that if you want to know how well you are doing, go spend some time with family. I have to say, this turned out to be a wonderful healing and transformational time with my mom.

So, I can honestly say that being guided to south Florida turned out to be a true blessing.

I can't say that I was thrilled with that first job, but I trusted my journey.

We don't always get what we want at first. Sometimes it takes a while. But it's important to pay attention to the pulls of your heart. It's the wisest part of who you are. It will always have your back and attempt to guide you to the places you truly want to be.

Please acknowledge your steps, whatever they are.

And if this analogy helps, think of God as your boss. You are the employee. When the boss tells you to do something, you do it because that makes the boss happy. Once the boss sees that you are doing a great job, the boss will give you even more "work," more responsibility. Before you know it, you are doing a happy dance from all the good happening in your life.

What do you want to create? What do you want to ultimately experience? How much money would you like to generate in the next three to six months? What would be a bit of stretch, but still somewhat believable? What would be your miraculous dollar amount?

Always take inspired action. You may not feel inspired, but you will know that this is what the next step is for you. It does not have to be a big step. Just remember to take a step, regardless of what its size might be.

The Universe rewards action with more inspired guidance and action.

One thing I know for sure: When you are clear where you ultimately want to be, it's possible to get there. You may not know how, but you don't have to. Leave that up to God and your Universal team.

It is never too late to create wealth...ever!

Dear God:

The struggles of life have worn me down. As much as I want to believe that I can finally create wealth, I am tired from the struggle of all these years of "trying." Please help restore my faith. Help me know that you are with me and are guiding me to the miracles only you can provide. I am your servant. I wish to contribute. I will listen. I will follow-through. I will share my gifts, my skills, and my talents. I will be forever grateful that my contribution has made a significant difference, and my assets reflect all those whose lives I have been able to touch.

Chapter 16

Your Results Accelerator

I no longer remember when I first had the idea that there may be a way to get even better and faster results. When working with a specific issue, I had already shifted my emphasis on creating and focusing on your outcome, what you ultimately wanted to achieve or experience. The focus is on your future—the future you want to create, live, and experience.

Using the Miraculous Living Method, you are also able to infuse into your mind empowering beliefs and scenarios. In working this way, the interference and limitations that were created from the past are literally washed away. The mind is now trained and strengthened to be in alignment with what you want to create, experience, and achieve. It was a game-changer.

But I had another idea.

What if there was another way to influence someone's outcome? I had already been creating life from 10 specific areas, referring to them as Your Wheel of Life. And one day—I don't remember what had me do this—I "muscle tested", using applied kinesiology to see if one of these areas would accelerate the outcome of whatever result we were focusing on.

Let me give you an example of one of the first times I tried this out.

Bob was a consultant. We had met several years earlier at a conference. Bob had now gone through a divorce and had moved from south Florida to Costa Rica. When he phoned me, he expressed concern, since his business had lost traction and his income had significantly declined.

Using my Results Accelerator process, Bob's entry point—the area that he needed to focus on first to get his business and finances back in flow—was to date!

Now, you need to know, if it were up to me, using my mind and the way I think, I would not have recommended that. However, I had learned to trust my guidance. So, even though Bob was a bit perplexed by my recommendation, he was willing to give it a try.

He got online and began connecting and talking with different women. Within a very short period of time, he connected with a woman in Brazil. He felt they had a really great connection and there was mutual interest.

This all happened in a matter of 3 weeks.

And what was even more interesting, Bob suddenly was offered a generous contract. In fact, Bob's business began growing again. Then, after approximately 3 months, Bob chose to move to Brazil to begin a life with this woman. Due to the way he was able to work remotely, he could live anywhere and still provide quality service to his clients.

In many ways, I was both surprised and pleased how this worked. I was being shown, once again, that when we surrender to a higher power, your Inner Wisdom, you are always guided to your best outcome and life.

Beth is another example. Beth was referred to me by her good friend Lin, who had previously worked with me. Lin had come to me since she was 60 pounds overweight and was unable to lose it. Lin responded really well to the Miraculous Living way to lose weight. Her first month, she lost 20 pounds. She lost another 20 pounds her second month. And, ultimately, she lost 60 pounds and was able to get off all of her medications except one.

Now, Beth wanted similar results.

By now, I was using the Results Accelerator.

In Beth's case, her Results Accelerator was she was to first focus on her career. When I shared this with Beth, she was not happy with me. She came to me to release her excess weight, not talk about her career.

However, once I explained a little more, our conversation shifted.

It turns out that Beth was really unhappy with her current job. Although we were still going to focus on her health, it was going to be important that we also focused on the possibility of her finding a new job.

I shared with her that I never knew *why* someone was guided to begin a certain way; however, I had learned to trust the process. And I encouraged Beth to do the same.

So, she began looking at what jobs might be out there. In a matter of 3 weeks, Beth found a new job.

And what was even more wonderful? After she began her new job, the pounds started to melt off her body!

Simply amazing.

I have used this part of my system in a variety of ways, although the most common are making more money, attracting love, and improving health/losing weight.

I remember doing the Results Accelerator exercise at one of my speaking engagements. I looked down and saw a man whose eyes were as big as saucers. I asked if he was willing to share what was going on for him.

He had been struggling with his business and was working many hours trying to get things in a more profitable position. His Results Accelerator was family. It turns out he was spending a lot of time with his work and missing being with his family. I encouraged him to do a little experiment: to carve out more family time in the next two weeks and see if he noticed any changes with his business.

He reached out to me about a month later, stating that he had been leaving his office earlier, spending more time with his family, and his business was showing very strong improvements in orders received. He was feeling more confident about the future.

In his case, he was being nourished by the love of his family, which somehow was resulting in the growth and profits of his business.

Even though he thought he was taking care of his

family by working harder and harder, he was able to experience how his family provided a wealth of love and happiness, taking *that* back into his company.

So, this is a way to get easier, faster results.

WANT TO FIND OUT WHAT YOUR PERSONAL RESULTS ACCELERATOR IS AND AN EXPLANATION OF EACH?

PLEASE FOLLOW THE LINK BELOW

https://WendyDarling.com/MiraculousLifeBook

Did you do it?

I would encourage you to repeat this exercise periodically, since your Results Accelerator can change over time.

Regardless, enjoy the process and see how your future action steps become easier and you begin experiencing better results. Not everything may materialize instantly (or they might!), but this will definitely assist you to make better, easier progress.

Dear God:

I am forever grateful to have discovered another way to accelerate my desired results. I am delighted how I'm discovering that achieving this can be easier than ever before. I can feel the inner stirrings of hope and happiness inside of my heart. I look forward to seeing how this all unfolds. Thank you for your continued love and guidance. I am on an amazing journey of creating a miraculous life.

Chapter 17

Are You Making Magic or Are You Making Mischief?

I love this chapter. I have somehow avoided writing this chapter until it was one of the last ones to write. Is this my mischief-maker making me aware that it is still alive and well? Is it coincidence? Well, we'll never know, but I do know we all have those little "critters" lurking in our subconscious. But I also know we have much more "magic" that can override them.

It has taken me much longer to write this book than my first one. I had more learning and growing to do while writing this book. We also were going through some challenging times in our world, with the continuing challenge of the COVID-19 pandemic. In addition, my son went through a significant health challenge, which captured my heart and attention. And I'm happy to say that he's now doing much better and on the road to a full recovery.

So, there were times it was easy for me to write. There were times it was easy for me to believe in miracles and living a miraculous life. And there were many, many times when I questioned if I had become delusional, since my life was not feeling the least bit miraculous.

But I can also tell you, I had the miracle of an amazing partner, John, supporting me during those initial weeks with Adam, my son. I truly recognized, without a question or doubt, the incredible friends I am blessed to have. And my two sisters were right there for me as well.

Since I had always done a really good job of being there for others, this was a unique time for me to receive their love and support. I was like a dry sponge, taking it all in. And I felt amazing gratitude to be blessed with such incredible people in my life.

But with the stress and worry during my son's illness, my body became extremely fatigued. I had been going through such an unusual period of time, as I've already mentioned. I had lost the "oomph" with my work. I knew something was brewing inside of me and I was being guided to cocoon and spend more time in quiet. So, my business slowed a bit and I allowed it to. And then the pandemic hit, and my business slowed a bit more. Clients were still showing up; however, my schedule was lighter than normal. But that turned out to be a miraculous blessing, freeing my time to focus on my son.

I share this with you, since I could have easily concluded that I was creating mischief. I was not being my normal, productive self. I can also share that there were moments that I wondered if I was just fooling myself and had just become lazy.

But the reality is that everything worked out just perfectly.

And there are times we do create mischief.

You know what I mean, don't you? You need to be working on a project and you find yourself getting up from your desk, getting something to eat or drink. You find yourself scanning social media or your emails. You suddenly have the urge to clean your desk, your books, your files, your closet, your whole house. I've had moments where everything was sparkling.

You get the general idea.

It's the moments that you decide you are going to do something, and you simply do not do it. You may not even realize at first that you have been diverted by those little mischief-makers. And we have a whole bunch of them.

But there are ways to identify and tame them.

One thing I want you to know is that your mischief-makers are actually doing what they believe is their job to keep you safe. To keep you living within your comfort zone. They are not trying to be bad. It's just what they do.

EXERCISE: What is the #1 desire that you want to experience? What is your Results Accelerator? What are the top one to three steps you know you need to take to get yourself in action (remember, the Universe *loves* action)? What will it take for you to take that first step? When will you do that? Now, schedule a time (in writing) to incorporate your step(s).

Were you able to take that step? Did you notice any resistance? Did you notice yourself doing anything that kept you from actually taking that step?

Take a look at your past behaviors. Do you have a tendency to procrastinate? Are there ways you sabotage yourself, your steps?

These are your mischief-makers.

Make sure you go to Chapter 19, *My Favorite Miracle Making Practices,* and see what you can do to quiet those mischief-makers. Don't expect perfection, but do expect miraculous success.

For now, I suggest you write in your journal, addressing your mischief-maker(s). See what they have to say today. Dialogue with them. You can educate them. They are just a bit misguided and, instead of creating mischief, they could be become your vehicle to create some magic instead.

Dear God:

I know there is so much more I could be accomplishing. I am not sure why I get in my own way of making better progress. Help me be clear about what my next steps are. Help guide me to take those steps with ease and speed. And if one of my mischief-makers happens to show up, please fill me and my mischief-maker with love, knowing you are always loving and guiding me each and every step of the way. I am forever grateful.

Chapter 18

When Doubt and Disappointment Creep In

I can remember one Sunday morning, several years ago, waking up, feeling "something." I wasn't even sure what this feeling was. It was a feeling I had not labeled before. I had felt sadness a lot in my life, but this was not sadness. This was different.

I eventually wondered and figured it out. I discovered I was feeling disappointed in myself.

I knew I needed to dig further. I needed to find the part of me that was disappointed and not feeling proud of myself, where I was also needing more love and support.

My business had slowed down a bit. I was also finding it hard to muster up the energy to take the steps that I knew I needed and wanted to take. And because this was not typical of me, it was catching my attention. I was concerned.

I knew there was so much more I wanted to do, so much more I wanted to contribute. I was smart enough to know that I had some mischief-makers in my subconscious programming that were holding me back. I knew there were buried emotions trying to get my attention.

When I started to investigate, I first felt a place in me that didn't feel supported. I tapped into the hurt and anger of not having my dreams fulfilled. Then, I got in touch with the sadness of not having a loving partner with whom to share my life and the support that comes with that. I was feeling the sadness of working all these years with my business but wanting to be accomplishing more. I guess I was feeling sorry for myself, which was not typical of me.

I love what I do. I love what I can offer. And I love the results my clients get.

Yet, here I was, stuck in something.

And what I found shocked me. I found that there was a

place within me that did not believe my dreams could come true.

Seriously? *Really?*

That's what I do for a living! Whether personal or professional, I assist individuals and businesses to fulfill their dreams, to get the results they want. I assist them in living miraculous lives while living the life of their dreams.

And I have been doing this for a very long time (at the time of writing my book, this is the beginning of my 40th year since starting my business)!

The reason I share this is if you are feeling the fatigue of life, if you are wondering what needs to happen, if you are wondering if you can even find the energy to take another step...

I'm definitely here to say that you can do it, and it's never too late!

So, what can you do?

First of all, you need to honor your feelings. If you are sad, please feel the sadness. If you are lonely, please allow yourself to feel your loneliness. If you are disappointed, feel that. You don't have to know what the feeling means or where it came from. I have found over the years that giving attention and voice to your feelings can be extremely healing.

EXERCISE: Writing to the feeling is a very effective tool. For example, if you are feeling sad, ask your sadness to share what it wants you to know. When you do this, you write what you are feeling first and what you would like to know. Specifically ask the emotion you are feeling—for example, sadness—what it is wanting and/ or needing you to know. You may be surprised what comes out of your pen.

For example, I remember a client was having food cravings. Normally she doesn't have them, so she did not understand what was happening to her. So, she wrote to the part of her that was craving "something," that looked like food.

What came out of her writings was interesting. This part of her was craving love. And there was a protective part of her that wasn't allowing her to feel or even recognize the sadness.

And it can be rather common for this to occur. Remember how I was speaking that there are parts of your personality that want to keep you safe? Well, this is what is happening when you try to push your emotions away. There is a part of you that does not feel safe. You think that if you feel whatever this emotion is, you will fall into a deep hole and not be able to pull yourself out. Or, this could just be the concern that if you feel this feeling, it breaks open the dam of all these other emotions you have kept buried within.

The truth is that we typically have an internal mechanism that does not let that happen. That is why, if you feel you have a lot of buried emotion stored from your past, it is best to work with a practitioner.

However, when you are feeling something, I believe it is an emotion that is simply wanting to be noticed and acknowledged. To be given a "voice." For whatever reason it exists, it is serving a purpose, and it's best for you to discover what that is.

Lean into the feeling, take some deep breaths. By honoring the feeling, you are actually breathing those feelings away.

So, please hold these moments as gifts. Gifts to grow, to expand and open your heart and mind, and to receive all the good God and the Universe are trying to send your way.

If you practice this on a regular basis, it makes your life easier and more fulfilling.

You really are here to live a miraculous life!

Dear God:

There are moments I just don't know if I can keep going. I have tried for so long to be dedicated to serving others. I have dedicated my life to being the best I can be. Please help me know there is a better life waiting for me. Help me find the inspiration, the courage, and the strength to move out of this temporary time in my life. I thank you for all your support, especially in these times when I doubt how truly miraculous life can be.

Chapter 19

My Favorite Miracle
Making Practices

It took me quite a while to fully feel and experience my partnership with God and my guidance team. In part, because of my upbringing and my accident, I had blocked this amazing support from my life.

However, when I was finally able to surrender, open, and receive the flood gates of God's love and guidance, that was when my life changed forever.

I had intellectually known for a very long time that this was what I deeply desired. I knew this would make a huge difference in my life. And, bit by bit, I had gotten better.

Now, I am hoping that your belief system is in alignment with what I am about to share. More than likely, if you have come this far, it probably is.

Loving, valuing, and appreciating yourself is a fundamental and foundational aspect to living a miraculous life. And yet, it also can be a bit more challenging.

Here are some of my favorite practices. These are ways for you to take better care of yourself. These are also steps for you to incorporate into your daily life so you are keeping your physical, mental, emotional, and energetic body in alignment with the life you are creating and experiencing.

1. **<u>Caring for Your Body.</u>** We all know that when we have good health, everything in our lives is better. So, how are you caring for "the temple for your soul"? Are you getting enough rest? Are you listening to your body and feeding yourself foods that say, "I love you, body," or do you stuff your feelings, your stress, your fatigue, your loneliness, and disappointments with the kind of foods that push your feelings down? If you don't honor the feelings, they will be buried alive, never dying, until you are willing to free them. What are some ways you can show more love to your body?

2. **Spend Time in Quiet First Thing in the Morning.** Learn to take time to meditate, quiet your mind, and open your heart. If this is challenging for you, I recommend adding music. It helps to quiet the mind. What is it about your life that really matters to you? What is working in your life? What isn't working? What are you grateful for? What do you want to be different? Writing your thoughts and feelings on paper or in a journal is a very effective way of clearing your mind. This creates the opportunity to address feelings. You can explore ideas and focus on something that is creating confusion. When you do this, you are releasing the inner churnings, now creating an opening for easier and clearer ideas and decisions to be made. You may want to start by taking a few deep breaths, setting an intention for what you want to experience. How do you want to *feel* (feelings are very important)? Write out what you intend to accomplish. Continue to write anything that is bothering you or concerning you. Get it out of your mind and heart and onto paper. It helps.

After you have completed that, switch hands (the one you never use to write) and ask for guidance. This is where you can ask a question. What is your next best step? What does the Divine want you to know? When you use your non-dominant hand, it allows you to bypass your conscious mind and you are able to tap into your subconscious and your Internal Guidance System more easily. If you continue this practice over time, your conscious mind will begin relaxing and allow your Internal Guidance System to come through with ease. I can promise you, with time, you will be both amazed and grateful.

3. **Demonstrate Acts Of Kindness for Yourself and Others.** An act of kindness or love can be as simple as drinking a large glass of water when waking up. Of course, I'm a bit biased, but doing the Miraculous Living Method is always a good choice. Go outside and sit in the sun for 10 to 15 minutes. Go for a walk. Call a friend. Take a nap. Listen to some music. Dance. Notice and observe your thoughts. How kind are they? See if you can catch yourself if you are not thinking kind thoughts. If you catch them, you can speak to them, educate them, and change them. What are going to be your acts of kindness and love?

4. **Write Love Letters to Yourself.** We are familiar with couples writing love letters to each other. But I would imagine there could be parts of you that are starved for some love and attention. So, why not write love letters to yourself? What do you want to

hear? What have you always wanted to hear, but no one else has ever told you?

5. **Acknowledge What You Love About Yourself.** Have you possibly minimized what's special about yourself? Do you even know what those characteristics are? Start your list...now. And if you need some extra help, ask some of the people in your life what they value about you, what is special about you. Make sure you ask those who you can trust to provide you with positive answers. This can be an important step in loving yourself more. It's important to acknowledge what your gifts are, your skills, how you make a difference, and what makes you special.

6. **Give Yourself HUGS!** Too often, we are hug deprived. Come on. Try it. It feels good. If you have others in your life, ask them for hugs. I once read that 20 seconds of a hug promotes greater health, not to mention strengthening the connection with the person you are hugging.

7. **Give Voice to Your Feelings.** Your feelings are very powerful. They are a direct reflection of the thoughts you are having. Yet all too often, we ignore them. It's time to tap into the wisdom of your feelings. To learn to embrace them, no matter what they are.

I recommend you sit, get quiet, take a few deep breaths, and put your hands over your heart. If you have one of my sound healing audios, I suggest you play that. Other music can work as well.

a. Begin by asking: ____Say Your Name____, what are you feeling? And wait for an answer. You may be surprised how quickly it may come. Initially, you may receive feelings, such as sad, lonely, or angry. Over time, you may begin receiving more positive emotions, such as happy, hopeful, and grateful.

b. Whatever the feeling, recognize and acknowledge the feeling by saying, "I see you are feeling _____."

c. Repeat a. and b. (above) three times.

d. Next: _____Say Your Name____, what do you need?

e. Acknowledge what is being presented to you by saying: "I see that you need _____."

I recommend you do this at least one time a day, typically more.

The purpose of this exercise is to recognize that there is a part of you that has been disconnected and squashed. A part of you that has been hiding out but also keeping you from experiencing your life as a whole person.

By fostering the relationship with these parts of you, you are allowing yourself to develop and integrate in ways you had not been able to before, and you begin feeling a greater sense of freedom to be you.

So, I highly recommend you try this for yourself. It's a good first step for all areas of your life. And it's a really great step for becoming more in touch with your feelings and the desires of your heart.

8. **Take Time During Your Day to Take Several Deep Breaths.** Walk around, clear your mind, and ensure you are living from your heart. It is too easy to get caught up and your daily roles and responsibilities. Learn to take mini-breaks. Try setting your phone for 5 minutes before the hour several times during your day. This will begin training you to stay more present. We also tend to sit too much. This will help remind you to get

up and walk around. Standing desks have become much more popular, if that interests you.

Remember, it's important to: (1) Get in touch with your feelings and do the exercises daily; (2) Connect with and embrace your deepest desires; and (3) Create your affirmations of how you want your mind to be thinking and supporting you. With time, you can also create a scenario of how you will be living your miraculous life, the life of your deepest desires fulfilled.

With the Miraculous Living Method, you no longer need to identify limiting beliefs. The Miraculous Living Method trains your mind, emotions, and energy to be in support of your deepest desires being fulfilled while organically releasing the negative charge of anything that is interfering with that happening.

My deepest desire is for you to have your deepest desires fulfilled. For you to experience and live a miraculous life. So, I decided to offer you the experience and the gifts of the Miraculous Living Method. I've created Your Miraculous Journey Jumpstart to get you going. Just follow the link below for more specific details. Then, if you are interested, you can schedule Your Miraculous Life Journey Jumpstart session with me. It's one session, but we can accomplish a lot and I give you the process for your continued use.

https://WendyDarling.com/MiraculousLifeBook

Dear God:

I am forever grateful for the magnificent life you have gifted me. I am grateful for learning how easy it is to open my heart and finally receive all the love and support you have continued to shower me with. I am grateful to know that with your love and support, all my deepest desires are finally materializing. I am forever grateful for my amazing, miraculous life.

Chapter 20

Get Your Motor Going Again

I don't care how good you are; there are going to be times when you may lose your passion, your desire for whatever it is you are attempting to experience in life. It's almost inevitable.

I know it has happened at different times in my life. It has happened throughout this crazy year we experienced in 2020. Even as I write today, I found myself having to put more effort into moving forward. It took more energy to get dressed and go for a walk. I simply told myself to just go. I wasn't worried about how far I would go or how fast. The goal was to get out the door and just do it.

And that is what it sometimes takes.

While on my walk, I found myself feeling much better. The fresh air was clearing my head. The movement was good for my body.

Then, my schedule for writing today got disrupted.

However, I promised myself I would write, so it was actually perfect that this is the chapter for today.

It's not always going to be easy to take steps. But if you have decided on one step and take that one step, I think you will find that the next step will actually be easier.

It's just that first step that can be challenging.

I also suggest that if you are having to work on a project, whether it be personally or professionally, make sure you schedule the time to take care of it. I find having a structure, a schedule, makes it easier to do. Create both a starting time as well as an ending time. When you have a start and finish, it is amazing how focused you are and what can actually be accomplished.

Of course, having a coach or some kind of accountability partner is going to make it even better.

And remember about your mischief-makers, those little gremlins that are keeping you from doing exactly as you wish. Many times, mischief-makers are mistakenly trying to keep you safe. However, the key word is mistakenly. Take time to notice how you make mischief in your life. And learn to take tiny steps to shift those patterns. It's possible. It's always possible. And with the Miraculous Living Method, it can happen with greater ease and speed.

If you are really having trouble getting your motor going, this is the time to ask for help. We all need support. And there are times that receiving support is most important.

I want you to contemplate these two questions:

1. *How does it feel when someone asks for your help? How does it feel after you have provided that for them?*

   If you are like most, it feels pretty great, right?

2. *Would you want to deprive someone else of having that same positive experience by not letting them support you?*

I hope you are letting that last question sink in. Sometimes allowing others to support you is actually a gift for them as well.

You will continue to learn how to navigate all of this as you continue to create your miraculous life. You will know when you need to push yourself a bit. You will also recognize when you need to take a little time out to regroup. Learn to pay attention to the inner pulls of your heart. They are there to guide you every step of the way.

Then, be willing to take that next step, no matter what it may be.

Dear God:

This journey feels too challenging at times. I find myself running out of hope, running out of steam. I truly want to experience the miracles life has to offer. Continue to guide me. Continue to fill me with hope and inspiration. And help me know my next step. And, most important, help me see this miraculous life I have been given to experience.

Chapter 21

Living from Your Heart's Desires

Turning your dreams into reality is rarely a straight, easy path. You will feel inspired at times. Other times, you will feel discouraged. You may find yourself taking positive, even inspired actions. Then, you may find yourself not taking any steps at all.

So, I want you to expect the unexpected. I want you to love yourself during the process, since this is such an important component to manifesting your deepest desires. It's going to take patience and perseverance.

It's going to take practice to drop into and live from your heart. To feel your desires. It has you connect with your truth. And when you live from your heart, you will live with greater certainty that all your desires are, in fact, your truth—soon to become your reality.

As I now look back at my life, I am in awe of the perfection of it all. I believe I was to know what it felt like to not have my deepest desires be fulfilled at a young age. It allows me to offer the kind of compassion, inspiration, and support that so many people need today. And to be able to authentically say "it's never too late" is a message I believe many people need to hear.

But, as I have said before: You are never to give up... ever!

You may need to keep building your faith muscle. You need to stay open and recognize how miraculous your life actually is...now. You may also need to assess if you are heading in the right direction or in need of adjustments.

Do your best to enter and experience the gentle flow of your life. Know when action is required and take it. Know when you need to slow down. Even recognize when you are being guided to pause. The caterpillar should never break out of its cocoon prematurely. It can be rather messy. Discover your personal rhythm of life and enjoy the journey. When doing so, what you can birth is simply amazing.

This is why living from your heart's desires becomes so very important. You need to tap into and feel the life you are materializing. You need to walk around with faith and certainty, "as if" it already is happening.

When you want miracles to show up in your life, you need to feel those miracles and believe in those miracles, right now, as if they are already true. In fact, they are. They just have not yet materialized in physical form.

Stop asking God over and over for your miracle. It's already your truth. It's already on its way. Feel it. Believe it. Know it.

I cannot stress how important that last paragraph is. It's the difference between wanting something and actually having it.

If you feel it's challenging to live from that place, this means you have some additional inner work to do. The doubters that live within you are creating interference from that happening.

I know this is not the easiest thing to do, but it is a critical step.

You can do this! I know you can.

And remember, no matter how long it takes, it is your

truth if you truly desire it. But you must practice daily your belief and knowing that your heart's desire lives within you right now. And turning that desire into reality is also possible.

And if you want more support, reach out to me.

Dear God:

My heart of hearts tells me that this desire within me is my truth. Help restore my faith. Allow me to feel this truth in every moment of my day. And if I forget, help me to remember. I give thanks for all the blessings in my life. And I give thanks for all the blessings that are still coming my way. I give thanks for the blessings of my deepest desires being fulfilled now.

Chapter 22

Living Your Miraculous Life

"You know what the issue is with this world?
Everyone wants a magical solution to their problem,
and everyone refuses to believe in magic."
~ Alice In Wonderland

It's a new day. And it's a new time. There are ways you can begin living that will result in you being happier, healthier, and wealthier.

You can tap into and utilize the gifts of the Universe. It's unfortunate that some label this as living a "woo woo" type of life. But I'm going to say that this is the most grounded, real, happy, and productive way of living I have ever experienced. At this point, I would not know how to live any differently.

Now, it's your turn. It's your time. And your time is now!

I mentioned my former client Lisa, who passed away at the young age of 49 from cancer. From her story, we never know how much time we really have. I have witnessed too many people that have closed themselves off from life, from love, from happiness. The heartaches of the past are keeping them as a prisoner of their own life.

You have the opportunity of living a better way.

Gone are the days of working yourself to the bone, and still not reaping the rewards of your effort. I'm not saying you will not have to work, but when you follow the principles I've laid out in this book, you will be amazed how much happier you are, how healthier and energetic you will feel, how you are able to be more productive, and how your heart is overflowing with all the blessings you are experiencing.

Life truly is miraculous. *In so many ways.*

Have you started noticing more of the magic that life has

to offer? Are you beginning to recognize the multitude of blessings that surround you each and every day?

The miracles of your life are waiting for you, trying to get your attention. Are you taking time to get quiet? To notice? To open your heart, mind, and arms to receive?

It's time that we live more from our hearts. Let your heart become your first brain. Learn to feel when something is right. Learn to feel when there is hesitation or even a feeling to pause. Just this morning on my walk, I received a text from a client. She was to meet today with a potential business partner. On the surface, this potential partner looked very good. He has had years of success. However, her heart, her intuition, kept trying to get her attention. When she stopped and really listened, she sensed exploring this partnership was not a good decision. She canceled her meeting.

She may never know why she was being guided not to partner with this person, but she trusted her intuition. She also recognized that she had two other individuals who she had great respect for who were offering their support. When she looked even closer, she was amazed at how many people were surrounding her and supporting her.

Is there something that you might be missing? Please take time to appreciate the people in your life. Please take time to appreciate yourself. Continue to open your heart and your mind to receive. Reach out and ask for support. We are not to walk our journeys alone.

And I encourage you to keep notes of your blessings. I encourage you to keep a journal of the miracles that show up in your life. To experience a miraculous life, you need to recognize and appreciate all the miracles in your life. How are you going to begin looking through the lens that everything is a miracle?

I believe that as we begin looking at everything as miracles, you'll keep seeing more and more miracles. And, as you keep recognizing more and more miracles, guess what happens? Yep! You begin receiving more and more miracles. Some small, some large. Guess you get to find out.

So, how are you going to begin to embrace a more heartfelt way of living? I'm not saying to let go of your mind. That's impossible. The mind never stops. It loves being involved. Your job is to get your heart and mind to become best friends, so they are in alignment and working together.

Here are my final suggestions:

1. **Be very clear** about what you truly want to experience in your life. Now, pick the one or two experiences that are most important.

2. **Use the Results Accelerator** process to determine what area you need to focus on first, still including your other priorities. Trust the process. What's most important is that you take some action, no matter how small.

3. **Use the Miraculous Living Method.** This is where the magic can happen. Create your scenario of the life you want to be living. You'll listen to the audio and download the package of Transformational Healing Cards, placing your hands on the cards. Then, you'll say your scenario out loud, taking breaths after each sentence. This is going to help rid you of the internal interference while strengthening your mind to be in support of your desires. In addition, this will make it easier for you to feel the truth of your desire. And I will personally assist you with all of this. If this is of interest, please follow the link below for more information on the **Your Miraculous Life Journey Jumpstart offer.**

https://WendyDarling.com/MiraculousLifeBook

4. **Keep a miracle journal**. Take note of all the miracles you are experiencing in your life. To begin, you may have to stretch a bit as to what you call a miracle. Maybe not. See the steps you take as miracles. Recognize the multitude of blessings that surround you each and every day. These are all miracles. When a new client shows up: miracle. When you take care of your body the way that works best: miracle. New opportunity showing up: miracle. New idea: miracle. Solution to a problem: miracle. Feeling happy for no reason: miracle. When we acknowledge the miracles in our life, we notice and receive even more miracles.

5. **Enjoy and appreciate your journey.** Living with gratitude each and every day allows you to more easily stay in your heart and be more naturally in the ebb and flow of life. Whatever it is you want, I can say with certainty that it wants you as well. Be kind to yourself in this wonderful journey we call "life." Of course, be kind to others. Live with a generous heart. And wake up each day with the thought of "I wonder what miracles I get to experience today?"

It has been a true blessing that I have had this opportunity to share my heart, my mind, and my beliefs of what it takes to be living a miraculous life. It is clearly a miracle that I am finalizing my last words for you.

This book was created with a lot of love. This book was written to empower you to have more hope, more faith in the possibilities of what lies ahead for you. I hope you felt that. I hope you were able to take in the truths that exist on these pages.

And my biggest wish and prayer is that each and every day, you know how very special you are and how much your life matters. You were created for a distinct purpose. You were born with special gifts that you and only you can share. Your journey has taken you to this very day and time so that you and only you can offer what lives in your heart and soul.

Set yourself free. Open your arms to receive the abundance of miracles that are waiting for you to receive. And enjoy and celebrate your wonderful journey.

I thank you for taking this journey with me.

And I hope I hear from you, one of these days, sharing how very miraculous your life is!

I send you love...

About the Author

Wendy Darling is the founder of The Miraculous Living Institute, a personal and professional growth organization offering presentations, seminars, retreats, and private coaching. Wendy is a recognized expert on navigating change and achieving your desired results. Her transformational system, the Miraculous Living Method™, provides the vehicle for achieving those results with greater ease and speed.

Wendy has over 40 years of experience as a business and life transformation expert, keynote speaker, master healing practitioner, management and organizational development consultant, executive, entrepreneur, and radio talk show personality,

Wendy has a way of presenting simple yet profound questions, ideas, and thoughts in a way that motivates her clients, but more importantly inspires them to action. She guides people to the core of their desires, navigating them to their best path to achieve their desired results. She blends traditional business ideas with innovative techniques and practical life skills.

Wendy has designed and delivered more than 50 seminar and presentation topics to well over

200,000 people across the United States. Some of her signature presentations and programs include: *LIVE LOVE LEAD: The NEW Formula For Ultimate Fulfillment and Success; Create Your Miraculous Life (It's NEVER Too Late); The Miracle of Attracting Love (for singles); More Money Now; Loving Yourself Lean; The ROI of Collaborative Relationships; Winning At Business By Mastering Your Inner Game.* In addition, Wendy has provided consulting and keynote presentations to some of the country's leading organizations. Wendy now trains and certifies coaches and practitioners in the Miraculous Living Method transformational system so their clients can achieve easier and faster results.

Wendy is a former contributing columnist for *Metro Family, Dallas Family, Today's Dallas Woman,* and *Today's Innovative Woman,* and she has hosted her own radio shows on CBS The Sky Radio as well as in Boca Raton, Fla. She has been featured in *Forbes* and other publications and as a guest on numerous radio, podcasts, and TV shows. Wendy is the #1 best-selling author of *The Miracle That Is Your Life.*

Wendy holds a Bachelor of Science degree in education, a Master of Education in counseling psychology, a Specialist's degree, and post-graduate work in

Management and Organization Development from the University of Missouri – Columbia. Clients have dubbed Wendy as their personal "fairy godmother" for her ability to help them live the life of their dreams.

You may reach Wendy at wendy@wendydarling.com or www.wendydarling.com.

Other Books by the Author

The Miracle That Is Your Life, 2014, Crescendo Publishing, LLC

Connect

Learn more about Wendy and all her unique tools and programs at:

http://www.wendydarling.com/
http://www.gothedistanceconsulting.com/

Email:
wendy@wendydarling.com

Facebook:
https://www.facebook.com/wendy.darling.8

Linked In:
linkedin.com/in/wendydarling1

Made in the USA
Middletown, DE
24 May 2021